To Star
Jazz,

Congratulations
on your engagement !!

Aim High!

Much love,

Bruce

Aim Point

An Air Force Pilot's Lessons for Navigating Life

Colonel Bruce Hurd, U.S. Air Force (Retired)

Aim Point
An Air Force Pilot's Lessons for Navigating Life

Copyright © 2019 Bruce Hurd

ISBN: 978-1-64184-134-4 (Paperback)
ISBN: 978-1-64184-136-8 (Hardcover)
ISBN: 978-1-64184-135-1 (eBook)

Library of Congress Control Number: 2019908984

Cover design by Cherie Fox at www.cheriefox.com

Printed in the United States of America

Aim Point LLC
140 Encinitas Blvd #148
Encinitas, CA 92024

For more information on this book, the author, and Aim Point programs and events, please visit www.colbrucehurd.com

To assist our military veterans in greatest need, a portion of all book sales will be donated to the Disabled American Veterans (DAV) Charitable Service Trust.

To my wife JoAnn (also known as Anya).

This book would not be a reality without you.

Your joyful, loving presence has inspired me since the day I met you.

I am a better man because you are with me.

And to my loving parents, who were my inspiration for this book.

Table of Contents

Acknowledgements

First, I want to gratefully acknowledge the love, advice, and support I receive from my wonderful wife JoAnn—I talk extensively about how amazing and intuitive she is later in the book. Without her devoted encouragement, I would never have started on my journey to complete this book.

I would also like to give heartfelt thanks for my loving children and grandchildren: My daughter Emily, my bonus son Justin (from JoAnn's first marriage), his wife Jeanette, and their two sons Tom and Dane. Each one of them is amazing, intelligent, accomplished, funny, charming, and every wonderful adjective I can think of. They all hold a special, irreplaceable place in my heart and I could not be prouder. And I give thanks for the newest addition to our family, Emily's husband Chris. Welcome!

Finally, I want to thank those who have given me invaluable editing help and advice as I completed this book: JoAnn, Justin, Emily, my good friend Michael Doyle, my brother David Cornell Hurd, my sister-in-law MK Mueller, and my author coach/mentor Tom Bird.

And I thank you, the reader, for joining me on this journey.

Preface

(Back row pictured left to right) My wife JoAnn, me, daughter-in-law Jeanette, JoAnn's son (my bonus son) Justin, our daughter Emily, with Justin's and Jeanette's sons (our grandsons) Dane and Tom in the front row at a family wedding in 2015

Writing this book has been a journey. I've wanted to put my thoughts into words for many years. I originally intended to write a book of stories about my life with most of my writing centered on my 30 years of experience as a pilot and officer in the Air Force. I didn't originally plan on my book going much further than friends and family.

As I got deeper into my writing, I noticed a focus on some major, traumatic events in my life. These events carried a large amount of shame I kept hidden from the world. This shame, this trauma, needed to come out. It needed exposure to the light, so I wrote about it.

I've never been a victim and never will be, so I looked at these events from the perspective of "What have I learned? What have I gathered from all of this that has helped me become a better man?"

After I wrote the initial draft of this book, I had the nagging sense of "so what?" I came to realize I had been using specific values and principles as guideposts my entire life, although I had never written them down. My life journey had also been all about the process of reinvention — the ability to move into new locations and new situations with radically different job requirements and succeed.

This is what the fifth part of this book is about — it's an introduction to the process of reinvention and the eight principles I believe can help anyone achieve what all of us want: a joyful, happy life. None of this is revolutionary. Philosophers, military/business/religious leaders, ethicists, and self-help experts have taught these principles for many years. What makes my approach different is that I believe each of us can use guided exploration and focus to improve in all these areas.

This excites me, as I see sharing my experience and knowledge as an opportunity for me to continue to contribute in a positive and meaningful way well into the future. I also see a much deeper exploration of these principles as the focus of my next book. And, sometime in the future, either in book form or as part of in-person or video presentations, I look forward to sharing some amazing, interesting, and funny Air Force experiences I had during my career. Like the time my navigator became lost over the North Pole and thought he might have turned us directly toward the Soviet Union. Fun times!

PART 1

COURAGE

Here I am next to my T-38 Talon advanced trainer at U.S. Air Force pilot training in the fall of 1978. I was a newly commissioned second lieutenant and all of 23-years-old.

Chapter 1

Falling Out of the Sky

Air Force T-38 Talon with its gear extended prior to landing. (military.com)

I almost died on that West Texas night of October 4, 1978. Instead, I found my aim point.

As I prepared to fly, I strapped myself into my supersonic jet, the Air Force T-38 Talon, and plugged my G-Suit into the aircraft's pneumatic system. The G-Suit prevented me from losing consciousness during aggressive high-G maneuvers, because it inflated to help stop blood from draining out of my brain into the rest of my body.

By this point in my training, I fully understood the Air Force wanted aggressive pilots. I was a good student. Just days before my flight I failed a training mission for being too aggressive. In my haste to rejoin the flight leader during formation maneuvering, I accelerated so quickly I flew faster than the speed of sound.

Since regulations prohibited breaking the sound barrier except under controlled conditions, my instructor marked me down for lack of airspeed control. While he told me why he had to fail me on that flight, his tone of voice and body language said "attaboy!"

I was a 23-year-old second lieutenant student pilot, doing so well the instructors chose me as the first in my entire class to solo at night in the T-38. Confident in my abilities, I had the procedures down cold. I made sure all my maps, approach plates, and flying equipment were up-to-date and readily available.

Once I settled into the cockpit and performed all my preflight checks that night, I started the plane's two powerful jet engines. I heard on the tower radio frequency they changed the runway because of a change in wind direction. No problem, I thought. Even though I had done all my night training on a different runway, I was sure I could make the adjustments I needed.

I taxied out and lined up on the active runway. After I received clearance for takeoff, I advanced the throttles to full power. When the engines got to 100% RPM, I released the brakes. The plane lurched forward, and I pushed the throttles into full afterburner. Since the T-38 has such short wings, it relies on speed to create enough lift to fly. When I engaged the afterburners, typically only used for takeoff and emergencies, raw jet fuel pumped directly into the back end of my engines. This created a controlled explosion that provided the extra thrust necessary for me to accelerate to my takeoff speed of 165 miles per hour. As I shot into the night, I felt like I could do anything.

After I completed an uneventful navigation leg around the city of Lubbock, Texas, I returned to Reese Air Force Base to do practice landings before calling it a night. As I approached the airfield, I requested authorization to fly an overheard pattern to a touch-and-go landing. The first aircraft to return to base that night, I passed above the takeoff end of the runway going 300 miles per hour (MPH). I pulled the throttles back to idle power and made a hard 180-degree right turn to set myself up on the downwind leg, reducing my speed, configuring my aircraft for landing, and getting enough displacement from the runway so that when I made my final 180-degree turn toward the runway I would roll out on final approach lined up to land the aircraft. Easy. I had done this hundreds of times already, even at night.

Except things were not what they seemed. No one knew about the severe wind shear between the wind at traffic pattern altitude (1,500 feet in the air) and the wind reported at ground level. On the ground, the wind went straight down the runway. At altitude, a 50-mile-an-hour crosswind pushed me closer to the airfield while I flew my downwind leg. This meant my displacement from the runway became smaller and smaller as I set myself up for my final turn for landing. It also meant the 50 mile-an-hour crosswind would quickly become a tailwind as I made my turn — I would lose one-third of my airspeed in seconds.

Since I hadn't flown a night approach on this runway, I didn't have any downwind ground references. The lighted electrical shack and the road intersection I had been using as visual checkpoints were useless. Still, I had general guidelines for where I should place myself and I used those. Those guidelines, though, didn't account for strong crosswinds.

As I reached my 30-second timing point past the end of the runway, I felt confident. I put down my landing gear and banked hard to the right. I turned my head around to pick up my aim point as I descended rapidly. The aim point is the spot on the runway that pilots use to make a safe landing. It's not marked on the runway. Instead, each pilot must determine his or her aim point depending on the type of plane they're flying, the weather, the condition and length of the runway, and a host of other things. Seconds ticked by.

Finally, about halfway around the turn, I saw my aim point on the runway. I instantly knew things were terribly wrong. I was way too low. Worse than that, I realized my bank angle was far too steep. I quickly focused on my angle-of-attack indicator on top of the instrument panel. It was glowing bright red. My stalled-out wings were no longer providing the lift I needed to stay airborne. I knew I was in a desperate situation. I immediately threw my throttles into full afterburner and raised my landing gear to reduce drag.

Because I had started my turn much too close to the runway, I had unknowingly maneuvered too aggressively, attempting to make things "look right" for the landing. I crosschecked my vertical velocity indicator and I saw it pegged at 4,000 feet per minute going down. My altimeter showed me plummeting through 1,000 feet above the ground. I wasn't flying any more — I was falling out of the sky. It would only be a matter of seconds before I hit the ground at over 100 miles per hour and exploded in a fireball.

My heart was in my throat. I carefully leveled the wings to increase lift. I needed to allow the plane to continue its descent to regain speed. If I tried to pull back on the stick too soon, I would lose what little lift I still had, and I would go deeper into the stall and crash. As I sank into the unlit darkness of the field leading to the runway, I saw the runway lights get flatter and flatter. I had to remain disciplined and continue my descent at full power just to give the plane time to accelerate to minimum climb speed. At one point I noticed the lights at the far end of the airfield weren't visible anymore because the small rise midway down the runway blocked them. The airfield was on a slight plateau and I was going below runway altitude. I knew I could hit the ground any second.

Looking back on this experience, I realize I was more afraid of failure than I was of dying. I didn't want to crash because I didn't want to shame myself or my family by the failure of not making it through pilot training. My father, a highly decorated World War II pilot, would never have blamed me for not becoming a pilot, but this would have caused him and my mother so much grief. To have their son die in Air Force pilot training would have destroyed them inside. And it would have been my fault, because I screwed up.

This book is about the traumatic events in my life. They all have something in common. They're all victories of mine. This is a book about these triumphs. It's about my facing disappointment, fear, and shame, learning from these situations, and moving past them. It's about how I applied these lessons and learned to navigate change in my life a positive way.

I expect any of you reading this book can identify events in your life you have been keeping secret. We don't reveal them because we fear the shame and humiliation we believe we'll suffer if people ever found out what happened. In this book, I'm shining a light on each of my "shameful" events, so they'll no longer have power over me. I'm freeing myself from living with the fear of being found out, of being embarrassed by what happened to me many years ago, often as a child. In this book, I also talk about going through Air Force pilot training — this is where the dramatic, nearly fatal experience I've described happened. Pilot training was ultimately a very successful year for me. It was also much more stressful than any other time in my life.

This book is far more than me reliving past traumas, though. Throughout my life, I've known I need to move past the pain and fear of these experiences to be the man I want to be and live the life I want to live. These shaming experiences, along with my stressful year in pilot training, also helped me recognize the goodness and support all around me. These trials led to my appreciation of all the amazing people and wonderful events in my life. The worst experiences of my life are also the inspiration for the guiding principles I used as an officer in the Air Force during my 30-year career. I discovered the importance of courage, compassion, integrity, and trust.

Just like all of you, I've succeeded and failed, and I've done amazing things. Along the way, I experienced situations and events in my life that have knocked me for a loop. Throughout it all, though, I haven't seen myself as a victim. It's just the opposite. All the events described in this book have been a co-creation. Whether consciously or not, I somehow brought these painful experiences into my life. The real challenge is to discover the benefits from them. What have I learned from going through each of them? What can I take forward to make the rest of my life better?

This is the reason for this book. I want to show how I turned around and even appreciated these traumatic events, common to many people, for what they inspired in me. I offer what I've learned from facing some very painful experiences. Much of how I applied these lessons relates to my experience as a career officer and pilot in the U.S. Air Force; however, I believe my insights may be helpful to many people from a wide variety of backgrounds.

Chapter 2

An Uncomfortable Silence

*My mother, Ann Cornell Hurd, and my father, Walter L. Hurd Jr.,
at home on leave during World War II*

My father was a brigadier general in the United States Air Force. Born
in 1919, he grew up during the Depression. He sent himself through school
at Morningside College in Iowa and joined the Army Air Corps in 1941. He
married my mother the day he graduated from pilot training, just months
before the outbreak of World War II for the United States. During the war,
he fought the Japanese in Australia and New Guinea before returning to
the U.S. in 1943 to create and train the brand new 314th Troop Carrier
Squadron, a transport squadron flying C-47 and C-46 aircraft.

After training his unit, he led them to England and France to fight the
Germans. He finished World War II as a 26-year-old lieutenant colonel — an
astronomic promotion rate for such a young officer. After the war, he and my

mother moved to the Philippines, where Dad and some wartime colleagues helped found Philippine Airlines (PAL). He started as PAL's chief pilot and rose to vice president of operations. In 1954, Mom, Dad, and my three older siblings moved to California a few months before I was born in December. Dad began his corporate career, eventually becoming Corporate Director for Safety and Product Assurance for Lockheed Corporation. He remained in the reserves until his retirement from the Air Force in the late 1960s.

During the war, my mother, Ann, completed her college degree in home economics at Iowa State and worked at an ammunition plant supporting the war effort. While she did some teaching when they lived in the Philippines after the war, once my oldest brother arrived in 1949, my mother focused on raising her family. In the early 1970s, she earned her master's degree in Special Education from San Jose State University. By the time I graduated from high school in 1973, Mom was an established full-time special education teacher at Quimby Oaks Junior High School in San Jose. Her students loved her. My parents remained married until my father passed on from prostate cancer in 1995. My mother was devastated, and she never recovered emotionally after my father's death. She died in her sleep in 2002. Devoted to each other throughout their lives, my parents are shining examples of the love and dedication a married couple can show toward each other.

They also had a serious problem they never came to grips with: my mother's alcoholism. Even after my mother finally stopped drinking in 1987, she refused to acknowledge the damaging effects on our family of her drinking and the pain it caused. Her denial was a perfect example of how our family dealt with the problem. We ignored her harmful behavior. My father discouraged us from talking about Mom's drinking and considered it disrespectful to even raise the issue within our family. Meanwhile, we were clear we should never talk about my mother's drinking to anyone outside our family.

We had another rule growing up: my parents wouldn't allow us to criticize each other. The intent behind this was noble — they wanted us to be a source of support for one another. Unfortunately, this also meant it was very difficult for us to provide well-meaning, constructive feedback to each other. This self-imposed prohibition on criticism had unintended negative effects on how my siblings and I dealt with my mother's alcoholism. Each of us in the family had to deal with this terrible problem alone. The situation was unbearable.

At the time I was growing up, American society didn't understand or accept the causes and problems associated with alcohol as it does now. People often viewed alcoholism as a moral failure to hide away from others, for fear of being treated as an outcast. As a child, though, I couldn't understand. Why can't Mom be the loving, wonderful mother I know she is? Why does she become this angry, hurtful, self-pitying person who I can't even stand to be around? I hated it when she was like that. I couldn't talk with her and I certainly couldn't count on her for anything. There was no telling when she would be this way. Was she going to hurt me? Was she going to hurt herself? Who could I count on? I could rely on Dad, but he works a lot and he's not always around. What if I'm home alone with her and she does something stupid or dangerous? These fears and questions haunted me my entire life.

Amazingly, despite my mother's alcoholism, in many other ways I had a stable childhood. My father, Walter L. Hurd Jr., was an executive at Lockheed Missiles and Space Corporation in Sunnyvale, California. The seven of us didn't live extravagantly, but I don't recall ever going without something important.

I grew up in Los Altos, California — a suburb of San Francisco. I was the fourth of five children, with just seven years separating my oldest brother Dave from my younger brother Kevin. Growing up in the Hurd family was sometimes a mob scene, especially with four boys involved. However, it was great to have ready-made teammates and friends, even with a heavy dose of sibling rivalry present. We were big into baseball and were huge San Francisco Giants fans (still are). Our lives revolved around schoolwork and sports.

I got my growth spurt very early and started shaving before I turned thirteen. By the time I turned 15, I was a freshman at Homestead High

School in Cupertino and I had grown to my current height (5'9"). I played football and baseball at Homestead, but only my first couple of years. By my junior year, my "adequate but not extraordinary" athletic skills weren't making the grade and the head coaches cut me from both the junior varsity baseball and football teams within six months of each other. While these were huge blows at the time, they turned out to be the best things that could have happened, as this allowed me the time to devote my energies toward other, much more productive areas.

I graduated from Homestead in 1973. Some of you might know this was one year behind Apple founder Steve Jobs, who graduated from Homestead in the Class of 1972. Our school had 2,500 students and Steve and I never crossed paths, nor did we have any classes together, so I clearly missed out on the opportunity of making friends with him. (I hear he did well.) After high school, I entered the University of California, Berkeley on an Air Force Reserve Officer Training Corps (ROTC) scholarship. Going to Cal as an Air Force ROTC cadet in the immediate anti-military environment of the mid-1970s was an interesting experience. More on that later.

For quite a while after college, I wondered what it would have been like to go to a university where being in officer training was a popular thing to do ... or even acceptable. In the years since my 1977 graduation, I've come to appreciate the excellent education I received and the exposure I had to a wide diversity of opinions and experiences I had at Cal. I've also learned to treasure my relationships with my ROTC classmates — the eleven of us remaining even make a point of gathering together every other year.

My wonderful wife JoAnn and I married in 1989. We have a delightful daughter, Emily, and also an amazing son Justin, from JoAnn's first marriage. Justin lives in Seattle with his beautiful wife Jeanette and their two wonderful sons Tom and Dane. I'll write more about JoAnn, Justin, and Emily later. I spent an incredible, very rewarding career as an officer/pilot in the U.S. Air Force and retired in 2007 at the rank of colonel. Because I had 16 different assignments over my Air Force career and I jump back and forth throughout this book, specific dates, places, and positions can be hard to keep straight, so I've included the details in Appendix A at the end of the book. After the Air Force, I worked the next eight years as a senior program manager at a large defense company in San Diego. I still fill-in as a consulting employee when they need my expertise.

Chapter 3

Connections with my Father

My father as a flying cadet in Army Air Corps pilot training in 1941.
He's third from the left.

It was 1984. I thought about my father as my crew and I flew our KC-10 tanker in and out of the clouds that surrounded the Owen Stanley Range. I was in awe of the jungle-covered mountains rising to 14,000 feet — I had never seen such rugged, steep terrain in my life. The Owen Stanley Range forms the spine of New Guinea, a large, still-wild island north of Australia.

This primitive, steaming, malaria-ridden land is where my father flew C-47 transports during the earliest, darkest days of World War II in the Pacific. When he arrived at the beginning of 1942, the under-equipped and ill-prepared Americans and Australians were fighting a desperate defensive war against a much larger Japanese force on the attack.

The Japanese launched a series of well-planned assaults throughout the western Pacific and eastern Asia, starting on December 7, 1941 with a surprise attack that decimated the U.S. fleet at Pearl Harbor in Hawaii. In the months that followed, the Japanese ran up an unbroken string of victories, overrunning Hong Kong, Malaya, the Philippines, the Dutch East Indies (modern-day Indonesia), and innumerable Pacific island bases, despite heroic Allied resistance.

By the spring of 1942, the Japanese already controlled most of New Guinea north of the Owen Stanley mountains. If they took the entire island, they could use it as an unsinkable base of operations to invade Australia and knock our ally out of the war. If that happened, an American counteroffensive would be nearly impossible. The Japanese would be on the verge of winning the Pacific war. My father and the other Allied troops in Australia and New Guinea knew they had to stop the Japanese even though no one had done it before.

My father and his squadron, along with thousands of other Army troops, left Pearl Harbor on November 29, 1941 on the U.S. Army Transport (USAT) Republic. The USAT Republic was a troop ship within a naval convoy en route to the Philippines. Halfway to their destination, the convoy received a coded message that the Japanese had bombed Pearl Harbor and our two countries were at war. The vulnerable convoy was dangerously close to Japanese-controlled islands. They were ordered to turn immediately toward British-controlled Fiji in the South Pacific and await further instructions.

On December 12, the Army ordered them to sail to Brisbane, where they established the U.S. Forces in Australia (USFIA), the first American military organization in Australia. After a brief period of training in Australia, my father became part of the 21st Air Transport Squadron flying C-47 transport aircraft (the military version of the Douglas DC-3).

Before leaving the U.S. in November 1941 as part of the convoy headed to the Philippines, my father started training as a fighter pilot. Once he arrived in Australia, the Army Air Force needed transport crews and aircraft to support the outnumbered soldiers who were already fighting the Japanese in New Guinea. For the next 15 months, beginning in March 1942, my father and his squadron-mates air-dropped supplies to frontline soldiers in New Guinea and delivered paratroopers behind Japanese lines.

They fought the Japanese in what can only be described as primitive conditions. They slept on the gravel and dirt ramp under the wings of their aircraft, draped with mosquito netting to fend off the hordes of jungle insects that came out at night. Their aircraft lacked proper instrumentation, and they used maps based on old National Geographic surveys — wholly inadequate for flying. I remember hearing my father describe how the American military was woefully unprepared when the war started.

Worse than the logistical problems, though, was the constant danger of being jumped by Japanese fighters and the ever-present threat of sudden Japanese air raids on their base. The Japanese knew they had to eliminate American airpower in southern New Guinea for them to win the war and they did everything they possibly could to make it happen.

On that day in 1984, my KC-10 crew and I flew less than 10,000 feet above the tops of the Owen Stanley Range as we navigated our way from Andersen Air Base in Guam to the Royal Australian Air Force Base outside of Darwin, Australia. We had to fly that low to stay within the Visual Flight Rules air route system. Even in 1984, there was no radar coverage where we travelled. We maintained our separation from other aircraft in our area by flying at even or odd thousand-foot altitudes (depending on whether we were flying northbound or southbound) and making radio calls over a common radio frequency at checkpoints along the route. We did this for hundreds of miles, just as aviators had been doing since they established the first common air routes in this part of the world in the early days of the 20th Century.

I couldn't help feeling a strong connection with my father as we flew above the rugged, primitive territory he had fought over during those grave days. I marveled at how he and his colleagues even survived the war, navigating their way through the narrow, jagged mountain passes of New

Guinea, flying as low as they could to stay out of sight of patrolling Japanese fighters. Such incredible courage and determination.

During that 1942-43 campaign in New Guinea, my father earned numerous medals for bravery: he was a three-time recipient of the Distinguished Flying Cross (DFC) and earned four Air Medals, also. Next to the Medal of Honor and the Air Force Cross, the DFC is the highest medal for courage in combat the Air Force awards.

In the middle of 1943, the Army Air Force reassigned my father stateside to train C-46 Commando pilots in preparation for taking command of the 314th Troop Carrier Squadron, a newly created squadron he would form and lead. With this new assignment he was promoted to major, a remarkably fast rise through the ranks. After training his men at Alliance Army Airfield in Nebraska and Pope Army Airfield in North Carolina, he and his squadron deployed in March 1945, to Royal Air Force (RAF) Barkston Heath north of London in England. Shortly after that, they forward deployed to Rove/ Amy in France. From then until the war ended in Europe in May 1945, my father and his men flew resupply and troop transport missions supporting the final Allied push on Germany. The day after the Germans surrendered, my father flew the first Allied aircraft into Norway. His C-46 was loaded with British paratroopers to accept the surrender of the German occupying forces.

My father was stateside, preparing to go to the Pacific Theater for the final major push on Japan, when the B-29 "Enola Gay" dropped the first atomic bomb on Hiroshima. The Japanese surrendered shortly after the second bomb dropped on Nagasaki. Millions of Americans, in the military and otherwise, breathed an enormous sigh of relief the war was over. They all knew an invasion of the Japanese home islands would cost an enormous number of American and Japanese lives. This would be on top of the hundreds of thousands of Americans who had already died over the previous four years of war.

My connections with my father have been numerous, and sometimes surprising, throughout my Air Force career. The most pronounced connection, of course, was both of us being pilots in the Air Force. Even though it could be hard to get him to talk about his wartime experiences,

Dad told us stories about going to pilot training as a young man who had grown up in small-town Iowa.

He described the shock of being thrust into the intense training and competitiveness in pilot training. He told us of his need to stand up for himself and the importance of doing the right thing. All of this I found to be true throughout my career, but especially in pilot training. It was a shock. It was intense, competitive, and dangerous. I describe that more in a later chapter. Throughout my experience in pilot training, though, I felt a connection with my father, knowing he had gone through something similar 37 years earlier.

As a young lieutenant copilot in 1980, my crew and I flew to England for a 45-day deployment to Europe, supporting air refueling training for Air Force aircrews stationed there. As we crossed the coastline and saw the green fields of the British countryside, I remembered my father and his descriptions of flying in Europe with his squadron during the war. I knew my destination, RAF Fairford, was not far from the same airfields from which he flew as a young commander. I could feel his presence with me in the cockpit, and I was honored to be an Air Force pilot flying in these same skies, just like he did. It was thrilling.

I could feel the strongest connections with my father as I dealt with some of the most difficult challenges I faced during my life. I remember hearing how, as the vice president of operations for Philippine Air Lines after the war, he stuck his neck out to train Filipino copilots how to be airline captains while his supervisor was away for an extended period. Up to that point, upgrades to captain had only been approved for white pilots, not the native Filipinos, even though many of them were highly qualified and had met all the experience requirements. It was not policy. It was just "the way things were done." It was also racial discrimination.

My father thought this unofficial policy was grossly unfair, and he did the right thing when he was left in charge. By the time his boss returned, Dad had trained several of the Filipino pilots as captains and the precedent for their upgrade had been established. Shortly after PAL leadership returned, they removed my father from his leadership position. While not given as a reason, everyone knew he was removed because he had trained the Filipino pilots as captains.

They reassigned my father to be a line pilot for the next several years, flying regular passenger routes in the Philippines and throughout the Pacific. It wasn't long afterward that my father and mother decided to return to the U.S., where Dad began a highly successful career in product assurance, flight safety, and quality control, rising to the level of corporate director at Lockheed Corporation.

When faced with difficult decisions, I would talk with my father to get his thoughts. Even after he died, his principles and presence were still with me. I feel as connected with him now as I ever have and I'm grateful to have his guidance. I am very proud to be his son. At his funeral in 1995, I delivered a eulogy that sums up my feelings toward my father. I've included that as Appendix C near the end of the book.

Chapter 4

Odd Bears

The amazing UC Berkeley Air Force ROTC Class of 1977 at our 20th Reunion in 1997. Pictured left to right back row: Lee Walden, Paul Pilipenko, Clint Gilliam, Bill Flanigan, Ray Nickels, Wayne Koide, and Rich Blomseth. Front row: Bob Gott, me, Adlai Breger, and Tom Dorgan. Not pictured at this reunion: Delores (Johnson) Street, Angelica (Rivera) Carson, Clayton Leitch, and Bruce Markovich

"How many babies have you killed today?"

The older student and his girlfriend glared at me as we passed on the street just south of the UC Berkeley campus. I was an 18-year-old freshman and living away from home for the first time. It was my second day of classes as a University of California Golden Bear. Walking back to the dormitory in my Air Force uniform, I had just finished my very first Tuesday morning ROTC training session. Even though I knew Berkeley was unfriendly toward the military, the anger my mere presence triggered in this student still surprised me. Over the next four years, I learned his response was not uncommon.

Air Force ROTC is an officer commissioning program conducted on well over one hundred university campuses throughout the country. ROTC is the largest of the three Air Force commissioning programs, bigger than either the Air Force Academy or Officer Training School. The ROTC program requires cadets to successfully complete 6-10 hours per week of classwork, leadership exercises, and physical fitness. This goes on for four years, along with intensive summer training. At the end of the program, with the recommendation of the colonel in charge of the detachment, the Air Force commissions the student as a second lieutenant. The new officer then goes to advanced training in his or her assigned career field.

The Air Force Academy is far more intense than ROTC and requires a complete, 24/7 commitment from its cadets. ROTC cadets can lead a much less regimented life while they're attending school. Apart from being far more familiar with all aspects of the Air Force right from the beginning, the biggest advantage I saw for my peers who graduated from the academy was they already had an extensive network of friends and colleagues as they began their career, while those of us from ROTC were just starting to make those connections. I also discovered, after only a few years into my Air Force career, it made little difference who graduated from the academy and who didn't. We were all evaluated on how well we did our job at that point.

I came very close to not even going into the Air Force in the first place. I applied to both the Air Force and Navy for ROTC scholarships — the scholarships paid the same amount. In the spring of 1973, the Navy awarded me a scholarship. The Air Force sent me a letter saying I was an alternate. Someone would have to turn back their Air Force scholarship for me to get one. I wasn't even sure if I was near the top of the alternate list or near the bottom, either.

Being a firm believer in "a bird in the hand...", I felt my decision was easy at that point — I'll go with the Navy. And I was perfectly OK with this. I saw the Navy as exciting and adventurous and I could become a pilot there, too. I also breathed a sigh of relief. As much as I adored, admired, and revered my father, I did not want to put myself in a position to compete with his achievements. By going into the Navy, I felt I could forge my own career, however long that lasted, and avoid any direct comparisons with my father's success.

For the entire spring and summer before I started college, I told my high school friends and work colleagues at the YMCA I was going into the Navy. I even walked across the stage at my high school's honors night, my proud parents in the audience, as the announcer told everyone I was the recipient of a Naval ROTC scholarship to UC Berkeley. I was all set to join the Navy. I was happy.

Then came the letter. At the end of the summer, the Air Force informed me it had upgraded me to a primary scholarship awardee. Someone had declined their scholarship. Perhaps they had a choice and went with a different service. Perhaps they received an academy appointment and chose that route instead. Or perhaps they decided the military wasn't for them. I never found out, and it didn't matter what the reason was. I now had a choice, and school was starting in less than a week.

My father volunteered to take the day off and go with me to the campus, about 50 miles away, where we could visit both ROTC detachments. We felt that would help me make my decision, and I appreciated his support. To his credit, my father never pressured me one way or the other, although I knew it would thrill him if I joined the Air Force.

As it turned out, both the Air Force and Naval ROTC detachments at Berkeley shared the same building: Callaghan Hall. The Air Force was on one side and the Navy was on the other. There were even two separate entrances, kind of like the dog and cat entrances at a veterinarian. While no one ever told us, we learned early on as Air Force cadets to always use the Air Force entrance. The Navy and Air Force weren't hostile toward each other. We just chose to operate in separate universes.

Callaghan Hall reminded me of a very impressive liquor store in a bad part of town. The building itself was stately and historic, but the doors and windows had metal bars on them. Those of us in ROTC were never completely sure whether the bars were there to prevent people from breaking in or to keep us in a contained area. There were frequent student demonstrations in front of our building, as we were the most visible symbol on campus of the military-industrial complex in the immediate post-Vietnam era. This intense anti-military feeling lingered for a long time, culminating in the destruction of Callaghan Hall by an arsonist in 1985, eight years after I graduated. That was a great loss. Callaghan Hall was an historic site, named after a Navy Medal of Honor winner, with an irreplaceable library dedicated to Admiral Nimitz, a former Navy instructor at Berkeley. Yet, ROTC never left campus and it's still going strong today.

My father and I arrived at Callaghan Hall the week before school started in 1973. He called ahead to let both the Navy and Air Force detachments know we would be visiting them that day. We went into the Navy detachment first because that was literally the first door we saw. A Navy petty officer met us at the front desk. Here's how the conversation went:

"Can I help you?"

"Yes," explained my father. "My son Bruce has both an Air Force and a Navy ROTC scholarship here at Berkeley. He's trying to decide which one to take."

(The petty officer looks at me. He doesn't get out of his chair and it appears like we're bothering him.) "He can come in next week with the other midshipmen and we'll tell him what he needs to know then."

Long pause.

"If you need anything else, there are pamphlets on the wall behind you." (Points to wall)

Long pause.

"OK. Thank you."

We walked down the hall to the Air Force detachment. We're met by a technical sergeant. Here's how that conversation went:

"Can I help you?"

"Yes," explained my father. "My son Bruce has both an Air Force and a Navy ROTC scholarship here at Berkeley. He's trying to decide which one to take."

"Oh, yes. You called, didn't you? Let me get Colonel Wasson." (Colonel Wasson was the detachment commander). The sergeant left to get Colonel Wasson, who walked out of his office, extended his hand to both of us, and we shook hands.

"Welcome to Cal. Very glad to meet you both. We really hope you choose the Air Force, Bruce."

The rest of the lengthy conversation went like that. Colonel Wasson explained the Air Force ROTC program at Cal and what I could expect as a cadet. He called the other ROTC instructors over and introduced them to us. Somewhere near the end of our conversation, one of the instructors asked if my father had ever been in the military — it hadn't come up previously and my father hadn't mentioned anything to that point. He pulled out his military ID that showed he was a retired Air Force brigadier general. That got their attention. They called over Major Post, the area recruiting chief, who happened to be in his office. He took my father and me into one of the classrooms and showed us a recruiting slide-show describing the ROTC program in more detail. After he finished, we said goodbye to the Air Force team, and they emphasized they hoped to see me at Corps Training next week.

Dad and I walked back to the car for the trip home. On the one-hour drive, we talked about the visit. Dad asked me if I had made my decision. I realized I had a very important choice to make — one that would affect my life profoundly from that moment on — and I didn't want to weigh first impressions too heavily. After all, my inclination had been to choose the Navy, because it had chosen me first. I also wouldn't be placing myself in direct competition with my war hero father and I had already decided I would accept the Navy's offer before the Air Force came through at the end of the summer.

Yet, the profound difference in attitude and atmosphere between the two detachments left a definite impression. I wanted to be someplace that wanted me. In the end that desire carried the day. I told my father I would take the Air Force offer. I could tell he was pleased. When we returned home and I told Mom, she was upset. It was because many of my parents' friends were pilots during the war and never came home. She wanted me to be safe on a ship somewhere in the Navy. Even so, she eventually came around and accepted my decision.

I've never regretted my 18-year-old self's choice, although I like to believe I would still have had a successful career in the Navy if I had chosen to go that direction. My encounters with the two ROTC detachments taught me about the importance of treating people well and how a first impression, either negative or positive, can change everything. It helped me make my life-altering decision.

I chose to attend UC Berkeley for many reasons. It had, and still has, an excellent reputation as a world-class educational institution. I wanted to receive a high-quality education from a prestigious university. As a California resident, I applied to a state-sponsored school that would offer lower tuition in case I didn't get a scholarship. Berkeley was also close enough to my family without being so close that I needed to commute. I wanted to live on my own without being too far away from home. Finally, I wanted to apply to a school that offered both Air Force and Navy ROTC programs. That last requirement narrowed the field down quite a bit. For example, the only two University of California campuses that offered both Air Force and Navy ROTC were UC Berkeley and UCLA.

What I didn't include in my decision was the atmosphere at mid-1970s UC Berkeley toward ROTC students. As an ROTC cadet, I found the immediate, post-Vietnam environment on campus ranged from indifference at best, to outright hostility at worst. Outside of my cohort of fellow ROTC cadets and instructors and a handful of close, non-ROTC friends, I don't remember ever receiving supportive comments or gestures regarding my ROTC activities from any students or faculty members during my entire four years on campus. I do remember snide remarks from fellow students like the one I described at the beginning of the chapter. Sometimes these encounters were confrontational, mostly they were not. I felt many of my professors were neutral regarding my ROTC participation; however, there were some who clearly appeared to resent my being in their class.

Dating a student at Berkeley was nearly out of the question. For one thing, those of us who were ROTC cadets completely stood out from all the other students. Apart from occasionally walking around in uniform — a dead giveaway — we were the only people on campus who had haircuts. We were completely out of fashion and easily identifiable. We found our dates elsewhere. I had a steady girlfriend from my hometown for about a year after I started at Cal — we broke up early during my sophomore year.

After that, despite having infinite charm and undeniably good looks (cough, cough), my dates were few and far between and never with another Cal student. This was not from a lack of trying on my part. Many of my fellow cadets had similar experiences. We were worse than nerds. We were social pariah "ROTC (pronounced 'ROT-see') Nazis." It was an isolated existence in the middle of a large campus full of students our age.

As a result, those of us in ROTC bonded. Not only did we see each other for hours per week over four years, we hung out together outside of cadet training. Many of us even roomed with each other off campus. ROTC activities and advancement within the cadet corps became an important focus. Just as important, we supported one another. We cheered each other's successes and offered help when things weren't going so well. By far, my most prominent memories of UC Berkeley were those times spent with my fellow cadets. We have even kept in touch with each other after Cal. While there are a couple of us with whom we've lost contact and, sadly, two who have passed on, the rest of the 15 officers in our commissioning class have been gathering at reunions since 1997. It's always so much fun to catch up with each other every two years to celebrate our lifelong friendships.

Chapter 5

Obstacle Course

Taking the oath of office at my officer commissioning ceremony in the Nimitz Library at Callaghan Hall on April 2, 1977. Our Air Force ROTC commandant at the University of California, Colonel Reagan H. Beene Jr., is administering the oath to me.

It was the spring of my senior year. My vision was blurred, and I couldn't do anything about it. I stood in line at my pre-commissioning physical at Travis Air Force Base and I was close to being called forward to take my eyesight examination. The situation felt hopeless. There was no way out.

So, this was how my dream of becoming a pilot was going to end? After all the selection boards I passed and training hurdles I jumped, I was going to fail the eye test mere months before reporting to pilot training? I needed time for my far vision to adjust back to 20/20, but it was too late. There wasn't enough time. I was just about at the front of the line and I knew I couldn't pass the test.

Then a master sergeant appeared from out of nowhere. I didn't even notice him until he spoke up.

"We need someone to take the electrocardiogram test. You. Come with me."

He didn't ask for volunteers. There was no time to even respond to what he was saying. He simply pointed at me. I jumped out of line and went with him. I knew this would give me time to adjust my eyesight. It was a miracle. This is a fairly long story, which I write about below, so just keep reading; it saved my Air Force pilot career.

Despite the enormous academic rigor at UC Berkeley, I never doubted I would graduate and get my commission as an officer in the Air Force. I just had to keep applying myself to the tasks at hand. What I wasn't sure about was whether I would even get into pilot training in the first place. By the time the spring of 1976 rolled around at the end of my junior year, the Air Force realized there were too many cadets lined up for pilot slots. Flight training had been slashed by 80% due to severe post-Vietnam War budget cuts. For my class (the Class of 1977) and the classes in front of and behind us, they cut the number of ROTC cadets designated for pilot training by 70% nationwide.

This meant that of the 1,000 cadets promised pilot training in my class, only 300 would be allowed to attend. The Air Force held a "reverse selection board" to determine which cadets would keep their coveted pilot slots. They ranked us from 1 to 1,000 in merit order and then took away pilot assignments from "the bottom 700." To put this into perspective, those 1,000 pilot assignments had been awarded to the 1,000 scholarship cadets who had been chosen from among 30,000 applicants across the country before we entered college in 1973. While there had been some movement in and out of the nationwide cadet corps from 1973 to 1976, the basic quality cut was the same. These 1,000 pilot selectees were the best of a very select group.

The cut was devastating. Six of my classmates, including my roommate, had flying training slots taken away. My other roommate, Rich, and I kept ours. We knew we were very fortunate. The two of us, and the other three cadets at UC Berkeley who kept our pilot assignments, had conflicting emotions. We were sad for our friends who lost their slots, guys we had come to know and become close to over the past three years in the corps. Yet, we were extremely relieved the Air Force didn't release us. It was heart-wrenching. In the end, the cut to 300 pilot candidates meant only the top 1% of those who wanted to become Air Force pilots through ROTC would even go to training. We knew we were damn lucky.

Because we knew this, we were acutely aware each of us had a slot thousands of other guys would have given anything for. This group included some of our best friends. We treated this opportunity with the respect and reverence it deserved. And for God's sake, we had to do our best. We couldn't allow ourselves to fail. Quitting was out of the question, regardless of how difficult things might get. Period. Failure would have been awful, but quitting would have been unforgivable. We had to keep going, no matter how tough it was, despite any of our personal desires.

Our wants and desires were completely in line with what we were about to do in pilot training. I wanted to do well because I had long wanted to be an Air Force pilot. Failing to graduate would have been devastating. I had to earn my wings, no matter what I encountered. I wouldn't let the Air Force intimidate me. They could send me home for not doing well if it came to that, but I would never even think about quitting.

Even after I made the pilot training cut and kept my assignment to flight school, there was still one more big hurdle to overcome before I could report for duty. I had to pass a pre-commissioning flight physical. Under normal circumstances, this wouldn't be a problem. Unfortunately for me, I discovered about halfway through college that my eyesight was getting progressively worse. To be a pilot, I had to have 20/20 vision uncorrected. It was clear the Air Force wouldn't give waivers to anyone who couldn't pass all aspects of the flight physical. I knew there were thousands of people who were ready, willing, and able to take my slot.

Near the end of my sophomore year, I took an eye test on my own initiative at the UC Berkeley optometry school. The results were not good. Because of all the reading I had to do, my vision was now 20/30 bordering on 20/40, much worse than the mandatory 20/20 eyesight requirement for pilot trainees. I was heartbroken. It didn't help that the optometry student who gave me the test told me, "Cheer up, maybe you can be a navigator." Knucklehead.

My father asked around and found an ophthalmologist in Palo Alto who specialized in non-invasive, corrective eye treatments. This was important, because I couldn't get any surgery or medical treatments without advising the Air Force, which would highlight my eyesight deficiency and cause them to remove me immediately from the pilot training list. Anything I did, I needed to accomplish on my own, without violating Air Force protocols.

At the end of my first examination, the doctor told me he could help. My spirits soared. He gave me a prescription for a set of glasses I would have to use anytime I was reading. These glasses would reduce the strain on my eyes and help reset my eyesight to my natural 20/20 vision. The catch was I would need to use them religiously for the treatment to be effective.

I found on those few occasions when I needed to read without my glasses, my far vision would blur almost immediately, and it would take 15-20 minutes to get it fully back to 20/20. So, for my junior and senior years, I would wear these half-glasses every time I read or studied, including in my ROTC courses. This caused my ROTC classmates and professors to wonder "what was up with the pilot candidate who was wearing glasses," but no one ever raised a red flag because I could still pass the eye test without them.

Fast forward to the spring of 1977. I am with a couple dozen Air Force ROTC cadets gathered at Travis AFB outside of Fairfield, CA for our pre-commissioning physicals. I'm confident I can pass all the tests, including the eye test, which is the first station. Then, they hand us a series of forms to fill out. The print is tiny. I don't have my glasses because wearing those would instantly raise the issue of whether I have 20/20 vision.

I have no choice but to press ahead. My heart sinks. I fill out the forms for the next 15 minutes and turn them in. I look in front of me and things are blurry. I'm now required to report to the first station and take my eye test. I go to the back of the line. There are five of us waiting, and I'm desperately trying to focus on things in the distance to make whatever improvements I can. It's no use. The line is moving quickly and there's not nearly enough time. I can't pass the test. I will fail the physical and lose my pilot slot. I feel terrible down to the pit of my stomach.

What happened next can only be described as divine intervention. There were two guys ahead of me in line when the master sergeant I described earlier directed me to take an electrocardiogram test. He appeared from out of nowhere and just pointed at me, like an angel of deliverance.

I immediately got out of line and followed him to the EKG station. They hooked me up, and I went through the battery of tests evaluating my heart functions. The entire time, I'm focusing on the ceiling, working on my far vision. My eyesight is improving. After 10-15 minutes, I'm released to take my eye test. I make a point of going to the back of the line even though the guys in front of me offered to let me go ahead of them since I had been pulled out of line earlier.

"No thanks, I'm happy to wait my turn."

I continue to focus on things in the distance. By the time I get to the front of the line, my eyesight has recovered completely. I pass the test with no problem. It was a miracle.

Because I never again had the extraordinary reading load I had in college, I passed all my Air Force eye exams from that point forward with no problem. Not that it would have mattered much either way. Once I was a trained Air Force pilot, if I had issues with my eyesight, I would be given glasses to correct my vision while flying. They just didn't want to send anyone to flying training who wasn't in top physical shape to begin with.

After having received my degree from UC Berkeley and completed all my commissioning requirements, including passing my physical exam, I had finished the obstacle course. I was now a commissioned second lieutenant with orders to attend Undergraduate Pilot Training as a member of Class 79-02. Pilot training started in January 1978 at Reese Air Force Base near Lubbock, in West Texas. As difficult as it was to get to this point, the hardest part was about to begin.

Chapter 6

Wings

Flying formation in the Air Force T-37 primary trainer over the West Texas prairie in the summer of 1978. I'm the pilot on the right.

"Room Ten-Hut!"

I was a 23-year-old second lieutenant student pilot at Air Force pilot training. All 19 of the students in my section jumped out of our chairs and stood at attention, eyes facing forward. The instructor pilots in our flight filed in and gathered at the back of the room while one of them walked to the front and stood at the podium. He addressed us. We remained at attention.

"You are in Muleshoe Area. You are near the end of your training mission. You look at your fuel gauge and you've reached bingo fuel. Time to return to base. Suddenly, your #1 engine fire light comes on. You look over your left shoulder and you see your plane is trailing smoke. What do you do ... Lieutenant Hurd?"

The other 18 students sit down. It's my turn in the barrel. They have chosen me today. I carefully responded to the scenario, reciting the precisely memorized procedures we used for specific emergency procedures. The instructor continued with follow-up questions to ensure I properly reacted to whichever way the scenario developed. Finally, after several minutes standing at attention and answering questions, the instructor told me I could sit down. I had passed.

There is no winning in this situation. If I answer the scenario correctly, complete with follow-up questions and alternative situations, I get to remain on the flying schedule. I'm expected to answer correctly. If I don't get everything right, I'm unceremoniously removed from the flying schedule, and I get a failing mark for the entire day. Worse than that, if I fail, I'm on my way to developing a reputation for being lazy, unprepared, and not able to perform under pressure. "Can this guy even cut it?" the instructors would wonder. It was a no-win situation —the best I could do was not lose any ground. This ritual went on every day of our flight training for the entire year. And this was only one of the many ways the instructors used to intimidate students.

Air Force pilot training was hard. It was in-your-face, it was relentless, and it lasted a full year. The Air Force designed it to put constant pressure on student pilots. Many of the instructors were hardcore, no-bullshit, Vietnam veterans in this all-male environment. Any actions or words that showed the slightest trace of uncertainty or weakness were magnified 10 times and shown to the entire world. There was a saying among many of the instructors that the best motivators for a student were "fear, sarcasm, and ridicule." It became clear that those students unprepared for the day's training flights, failed stand-up, or just weren't hacking it would get a lot more unwanted attention.

I wanted to avoid that situation at all costs. I did all I could to appear self-confident without arrogance and I wanted to look like I knew what I was doing. I made sure I studied hard, often with a group of my classmates, and that I knew all the required procedures well ahead of time. This would keep me from making any bonehead mistakes labeling me as lazy or stupid

— not that any of us in my class were either of those. More than that, though, I used my power of visualizing to put myself in a successful and positive frame of mind. And it worked.

I would go on to graduate from Air Force pilot training, one of the most intense courses the Air Force offers. It required my absolute attention for the entire 12 months. I didn't bring a television when I moved to Reese AFB in January 1978. Reese was just west of Lubbock, Texas and far away from where I grew up. I had just turned 23, and I didn't want any distractions while I immersed myself in learning how to fly. I felt sorry for the married guys because they had wives and children who needed attention. I could focus completely on my flying. Or so I thought. It didn't fully work out that way.

Like many other single guys, I dated while I was in training. I had a long-distance girlfriend, Jane, who lived in Southern California near my parents. She visited me twice, and I even went to see her on a couple of long weekends. We would write and call each other about once a week, too — long-distance phone calls were a major expense back then and we would schedule our next call before we said goodbye each time. Apart from my relationship with Jane and occasional get-togethers with my classmates, that was about it. I focused everything else on adjusting to the Air Force and learning to fly the way the Air Force wanted me to.

I had to devote myself right from the beginning. I knew this would be the first school I ever attempted where I could easily fail, no matter how much effort I put into it. Homestead High School was challenging, but there was never any doubt I would do well. I wasn't a threat to be valedictorian, yet I graduated with a grade point average and SAT scores that allowed me to get into the University of California at Berkeley on an Air Force ROTC scholarship. In no time after arriving in the fall of 1973, I discovered Cal was very different from high school.

I had to work my butt off to just get a C+ or B- in my calculus and physics classes. I loaded up on those during my freshman year as a physical science major. However, after one full year of competing with a whole raft of pre-med students, I decided I needed to change majors, or I would explode. I knew it would only get worse from where I was. I applied to the UC Berkeley Business School, which was an upper division school at that time. Fortunately, the school accepted me, and I graduated with a bachelor's degree in Business Administration in March 1977.

At pilot training, many nights before I went to bed, I used a visualizing technique bordering on obsessive compulsive behavior. I would lie on my back on the floor of my room in the Bachelor Officers Quarters. I would then throw a small, hard rubber ball in the air and catch it, throw it and catch it, throw it and catch it, etc., etc. I would do this for 10, 15, 20, 25, even 30 minutes. While I was doing this mindless, routine physical activity, I would visualize my flights the next day. I saw myself accomplishing each procedure and performing each maneuver perfectly. I saw how my flight instruments looked when I was flying. I imagined how it felt. I went through all the routine and emergency procedures I needed to know by heart. I had to know I knew it all perfectly because the physical aspects of flying the plane did not come easily at first.

As any teacher understands, people learn at different rates and in different ways. That's why good instructors have a bag of tricks they can pull out for each student. If one technique doesn't work, perhaps another one will. In pilot training, though, there's a standard curriculum taught by the instructor pilots. A student gets X number of rides to practice aerobatic maneuvers, Y number of rides to practice landings, Z number of rides to fly instrument approaches, etc., etc.

The curriculum doesn't consider the quality of instructor, weather conditions on a given day, condition of the aircraft, or any of the many, many variables that can come into play. The belief was that students should be able to get all the maneuvers down within a certain number of training flights. If they can't, they wouldn't make a good pilot and should be washed out of the program. This was theoretically a good method if we all learned the same way. The fact is some students, like me, learned the priority of inflight tasks slower and more methodically than others.

As time went on, I appreciated that what separates the best pilots from the others is an ability to absorb a wide variety of inputs and understand which tasks are most important — which of them need to be dealt with immediately, and which can wait until later. As I advanced in my Air Force flying career, becoming an aircraft commander in the KC-135 and an instructor pilot in the KC-10 tankers, I became an expert in assimilating inputs and determining a coherent course of action in a demanding military flying environment. This was a developed skill set. Some pilot training students who became accomplished military pilots take a little longer than others to bring all of this into focus. I was one of those.

Compounding the stress and difficulty of trying to succeed in this environment, I had a terrible instructor pilot to begin with. The squadron assigned me to an Air Force major on his last assignment before being forced to retire. He hated his job. He had been passed over for promotion to lieutenant colonel and was very bitter about it. He didn't take his responsibility to instruct me with any degree of seriousness. I was his first student, and I turned out to be his last. After the squadron became aware of his performance with me, they never let him touch another student.

His incompetence as an instructor was plain when I took my first checkride in the primary Air Force trainer, the T-37 twin jet aircraft. I failed the checkride so badly that I got more things wrong than I got right. This surprised the other instructors in my flight since I appeared to know what I was doing. It turned out the major taught me some critical procedures incorrectly, while he didn't teach me other important procedures at all. Because of the Air Force training curriculum limitations, I only had three instructional flights over the next two days before my required recheck. My new instructor, Captain Howie Price, did his best to straighten me out, but there was only so much he could teach me or correct in those three flights.

The first checkride in pilot training is the Mid-Phase Check (MPC). This is the one point, by far, where the most students fail out of the program. The MPC is where the squadron takes a critical look to determine whether they think a student has what it takes to make it. The MPC recheck, if it's required, is the place where the make-or-break evaluation happens. I knew if I failed the recheck, it was pretty much all over but the shouting, even though I would have one more checkride, the Final Progress Check (FPC).

If it came to that, we all knew the FPC was a rubber stamp and I'd be out the door.

When I failed my MPC, I found out people started shying away from me. They didn't exactly pity me, but it was obvious my friends and fellow students were glad they weren't me. It was almost as if they felt I was contagious and getting too close or hanging around me too much would cause them to "catch" whatever I had. Apart from Captain Price, the other instructors in the flight started to not pay attention to me anymore, since I'd likely be gone sometime soon. It was a terrible feeling. I cringe when I remember that period, kind of like reliving a slow-motion car wreck and not being able to do anything about it.

This is where my positive thinking ritual had a huge effect. Every day, I would walk into the flight room with an upbeat attitude and an air of determination. My classmates and the instructor pilots in the flight didn't know what to make of me. Typically, students in my situation had a "hang-dog" look and seemed defeated before they went to their last, failing checkride. In my case, this should have been particularly true since I had failed the MPC so miserably the first time.

To this day, I don't know if Captain Price or Major Leinen (our section commander) steered the squadron's check section into having Major Fry give me the recheck. I never saw any indication they did anything, but given they knew what occurred with my first instructor, they might have nudged the system to make this happen. Major Fry, the leader of the check section, had been around long enough to recognize what was important in this situation. He was there to determine my overall aptitude and attitude and not get sidetracked by whether I had all the procedures down perfectly.

I remember going to my MPC recheck with a determined attitude. I felt I was skilled enough to pass, and I knew all the procedures down cold, yet the disastrous experience I had with my first-ever checkride was just a few days old and hard to shake. I would do my best and let the chips fall where they may. Thankfully, while my MPC recheck was challenging, it was also uneventful. I performed everything within standards with a few minor critiques. Most important of all, I passed. I felt thrilled. I knew I had barely escaped a disaster. My classmates were happy for me, too, and I became one of the gang again. I wasn't "the guy who would be leaving soon" any longer.

I think I surprised more than one instructor with my success, simply because that was not typically what happened in these cases. I understand why their attitudes changed. I also attribute my success to the positive attitude I cultivated and nurtured. Without my complete focus on a positive outcome, I wouldn't have had a chance. It was shortly after my T-37 MPC recheck that things fell into place for me. It all came together as I learned what was a "now" priority in the cockpit, and what was important but could wait.

The Air Force conducted the advanced (T-38) phase of pilot training in a very different atmosphere than the T-37 phase. While pilot training remained oppressive and demanding, once we advanced into the T-38 phase the instructors treated us as if we had earned at least a little acknowledgement and respect. This was a huge relief. During T-38s, the Air Force's focus was on producing a qualified graduate and not as much trying to wash out those who didn't have the aptitude for flying.

The T-38 was a very different aircraft from the T-37. The T-37 was a conventional, subsonic trainer with underpowered engines; the T-38 was a short-winged, supersonic, high-performance, fighter-like aircraft. By mastering the T-38, we were proving to our instructors and the Air Force we were ready to take the next step and become full-fledged Air Force pilots. The T-38 also incorporated more advanced training than the T-37. For example, we had to pass a T-38 formation checkride involving two aircraft (a two-ship formation) and complete additional training in four aircraft (four-ship) formation flying. In T-37s, the Air Force only introduced us to two-ship formation flying.

The Northrup T-38 "Talon" began in the Air Force in 1962 and is still being used by the USAF today. Two pilots sit in tandem in the T-38, with the student in the front of the cockpit and the instructor pilot in the back. The T-38 was a major step up from the basic trainer, the Cessna T-37 "Tweet." It was much faster, and the instrumentation was significantly upgraded. It also allowed the student to perform like a single-seat pilot, with the instructor tucked away in the back of the cockpit, out of arm's reach. I really enjoyed flying the T-38, as it was fast, sexy, and performed like an airborne sports car. It was also far more unforgiving, as I learned later, with its short wings making it much easier to stall during the approach and landing phase.

Unlike my halting progress with a subpar instructor in T-37s, I had the great fortune of having an excellent T-38 instructor (Captain Chuck Hanner) right from the beginning. Captain Hanner was an F-106 fighter pilot who had received a follow-on assignment to be a T-38 instructor at Reese AFB — this was considered "a broadening assignment" outside of his primary area of expertise (F-106 pilot in his case). All career Air Force officers must do this. I did it many times, especially as I became more senior.

I was Captain Hanner's first-ever student when I started the T-38 phase. I was also his only student, to begin with. Because of that, I had his undivided attention as he got his local checkout and learned the ropes of being an instructor at Reese. This was a huge advantage, since I received focused, consistent training right from the beginning. Captain Hanner and I flew two or three T-38 sorties every day — a fast pace requiring me to be prepared at all times. It also helped reinforce skills I learned from one flight to the next.

Most important was Captain Hanner's attitude. Even though it was clear he would rather have been flying his beloved F-106 Delta Dart fighter, he was an excellent instructor and had a great perspective on things. I progressed rapidly through the program, soloed at day and at night in the T-38 earlier than anyone, and was the first in my class to take and pass the T-38 contact (flying skills) checkride. I also was the first, along with my classmate Steve Carey, to pass the T-38 formation checkride. Each of those were huge milestones in the T-38 phase.

In the end, everything turned out great. I graduated with my class in December 1978, ranking in the top one-third of my classmates. Both the T-37 and T-38 squadrons thought enough of me that they wanted me to come back and join their ranks as a flight instructor. While I was grateful for the compliment, by the time I finished my year-long adventure in pilot training, I didn't really want to return to that oppressive training environment. I wanted to find adventure elsewhere.

Chapter 7

Walls Closing In

Prisoner of War compound at survival training. (sfahq.com)

"Let me out!! Get me out of here!!"

The guy in the box next to me was screaming.

"Flight Surgeon!!"

One of my most intense memories in Air Force Combat Survival Training was having to squat in a tiny, pitch-black box with a bag over my head for what seemed an eternity. The box had adjustable sides that fit snugly around each of us, so we were touching all the walls as we curled up in a crouched position. I couldn't even move, much less turn around or stretch any part of my body.

It was then I discovered I suffered from claustrophobia. It didn't help that the guy next to me was having a fearful, claustrophobic experience. He had used the safe phrase ("flight surgeon"), which required the instructors to stop what they were doing and remove him from whatever situation he was in. It also meant he failed the course, likely jeopardizing his Air Force flying career if he was a crewmember. Successful completion of survival training was mandatory for all of us.

I could hear the instructors scrambling to get him out of the box next to me as he continued to yell. It was all I could do to maintain my presence of mind and not lose my own composure. This was the first time I ever felt on the verge of being overcome by this fear. I've only had three claustrophobic reactions in my entire life, none of which ever became debilitating. This one was the first and easily the worst. I felt my breathing become faster and get increasingly shallow. My heartbeat increased, and my mind raced as I fought off the panic. I had to go within and force myself to think about something different — I couldn't even acknowledge my situation to myself. I visualized myself elsewhere and shut myself down to what was happening.

To set the stage, after I graduated from pilot training in December 1978, I went right to KC-135 copilot qualification training at Castle Air Force Base near Merced, California in January 1979. I spent the next four months at Castle learning to fly the "Stratotanker." This was one of the most enjoyable periods in my early Air Force career. I remember the first time I saw a KC-135 flying at Castle. It was my first day there, and I was driving back to base after grabbing a bite to eat in Merced. I saw a KC-135 on final approach, paralleling me as I drove on a perimeter road. It looked big and sleek and beautiful. I realized, *I'm going to fly this plane, a plane that could take me across the oceans to adventures anywhere in the world.* It was love at first sight.

After graduating as a fully qualified KC-135 copilot in May, I went to land survival training at Fairchild Air Force Base near Spokane, Washington and then water survival training at Homestead Air Force Base at the southern tip of Florida — opposite corners of the country. Water survival was kind of fun … decidedly low key. It was more of a vacation than anything else. It was useful since we learned important aspects of how to survive if we either ditched our aircraft or had to bail out over the ocean. That said, the entire course was only three days in the south Florida sun where we did things like practice parachute landings in the water. Our final exam was floating around in a life raft in our flight suits within sight of the tourists on the beaches of Biscayne Bay. Not too tough.

The two-week survival course at Fairchild, however, based on the multi-service Survival, Evasion, Resistance and Escape (SERE) course, was no fun. After some brief classroom instruction, we divided into groups of 10-12 personnel and went on an instructor-led survival hike through the forests of eastern Washington. The one-week trek in the mosquito-infested woods was bearable, especially since I had been a YMCA camp counselor for four summers in high school and college and had done a lot of backpacking as part of that experience. I was one of only a few officers in my class and I was the designated section leader, which meant I got to try things out first. We didn't starve, and nobody broke any bones or got sick, so the training was a success from that perspective.

The mock Prisoner of War (POW) resistance and evasion training at Fairchild, however, was as miserable as it sounds. As a "senior officer," they singled me out for special treatment — more interrogation, longer time in the box, public humiliation, etc. The entire experience lasted a little over 24 hours, starting at dusk one evening when enemy soldiers (the instructors) captured us at gunpoint. We had no opportunity to sleep that night, as we stood at attention with bags over our heads, each of us in our tiny four-wall cell. They monitored and harassed us constantly throughout the night.

I still have distinct memories of the POW training experience. Even to this day, I can recite the words of Rudyard Kipling's poem "Boots" — the instructors played this on a continuous loop for hours, broken only by "news reports" accusing us of being war criminals. The poem narrator would get progressively more distraught as the recording went on as if he were going mad. It was disturbing to listen to this over and over and over. Throughout the night, the instructors would suddenly break the monotony. I remember being pulled out of my cell for a lengthy interrogation in the commandant's office, trying to not divulge any information other than name, rank, and serial number.

Survival training was a miserable experience, period, especially the mock POW camp resistance training. There's no way to describe it as anything else and I wouldn't try to convince anyone otherwise. Like all events in my life, though, I learned from this. I'm grateful I had this training. I knew if I ever found myself in a survival or, God forbid, a POW situation, I would appreciate having been exposed to this ahead of time. Hopefully then I wouldn't be completely overwhelmed by the desperate situation.

Despite the realism of the training, all of us knew we weren't truly threatened, and everything would be over in a short time. We also knew the instructors couldn't physically harm us, despite their threats and intimidating actions. Yet, the POW training drove home how shocking and frightening this experience could be. That was the intent. We needed to be familiar with what might happen if we ever found ourselves in a terrible situation like that. I can't even pretend to know what the brave men and women of our armed forces who have endured being a POW have felt. I can only marvel at their extraordinary courage.

I also learned, once again, that I'm stronger than I might have previously given myself credit for. That night when I felt the walls of the tiny, dark box closing in on me and my claustrophobic fears well up inside, I discovered I can be strong and overcome imagined fears by going within and focusing on something else. This knowledge has been useful throughout my Air Force career and in my personal life.

Chapter 8

Night Air Refueling

U.S. Air Force KC-10 receiving fuel in mid-air. (military.com)

I felt the sweat soaking through my flightsuit even though the cabin temperature was perfect. I had been on edge for 20 minutes. Focused completely on keeping the KC-135 tanker centered precisely 12 feet above and in front of my KC-10, we were taking on thousands of gallons of fuel through the KC-135's metal boom. These were the worst mid-air refueling conditions I ever encountered and there was no end in sight.

We darted in and out of the clouds going 450 miles per hour on a bright, moonlit night, maneuvering through the turbulence caused by thunderstorms only 10 miles away. The tanker had to bank sharply to stay away from the storms. Going from clouds thick enough to lose sight of the KC-135 into full moonlight created the illusion we were closing in on and about to hit the plane in front of us. Banking in a turn felt like we were becoming unstable with the increased G-forces, especially as we took on fuel.

The turbulence from the thunderstorms also gave the false impression I should pull back or close with the tanker to maintain position each time the storms buffeted us. I disregarded most of my physical senses to stay in position, keeping my complete focus on what I was seeing in front of me. I had to be steady and deliberate, regardless of what I experienced. I didn't know how much longer I could keep this up.

It was 1985, and I was a captain requalifying in the KC-10 for the 32d Air Refueling Squadron at Barksdale Air Force Base near Shreveport, Louisiana. Seven years earlier, perhaps the most important lesson I learned from pilot training, and especially on that near-fatal night in the T-38 advanced trainer, was the importance of courage and believing in myself. I have admired many courageous men and women, military and civilian, of all ages and nationalities. We all know people who are inspiring examples of courage. We encounter them every day.

Without courage, we sleepwalk through life, reacting to situations presented to us and responding to whichever way the wind is blowing. It takes courage to chart our own direction. That doesn't mean inflexibility. The most successful people I know work hard to understand and cooperate with others, which might mean compromising or changing perspectives. The challenge is knowing when to take a stand and when it's not necessary. I don't have any simple answers for that. Everyone needs to determine that answer for himself or herself. When confronted with questions like these, I've gone within to determine how I feel about a situation. While my responses haven't always been perfect, I believe I come up with a good answer by listening to my heart.

My KC-10 requalification happened right after I completed a non-flying tour as an Air Staff Training (ASTRA) officer at the Pentagon, spending a year learning how Air Force headquarters functions (which was fascinating). My requalification in the KC-10 involved an actual upgrade from copilot to aircraft commander at the same time. This required me to master some new skills as part of my training.

There are five phases of aircraft operations that can get a pilot in real trouble in the KC-10: takeoff and departure, approach and landing, tanker air refueling, taxiing the aircraft on a narrow ramp/taxiway, and receiver air refueling (receiving fuel in mid-air). Having been a KC-10 copilot and a KC-135 aircraft commander before I started my requalification at Barksdale, I had a good handle on takeoff, departure, approach, landing, and tanker air refueling — none of those presented a big challenge. It was a case of regaining a feel for the aircraft and re-familiarizing myself with the procedures. The first time I taxied in the KC-10 jumbo jet was difficult because of how high above the ground I sat in the cockpit and how far I was in front of the nosewheel and the main tires — it was a spatial perception challenge. Even so, I realized the worst that could happen in the unlikely event things went wrong taxiing was planting a wheel in the dirt and getting stuck. That situation would be severely embarrassing, but not fatal.

Receiver air refueling was different though. Unlike the KC-135, in the KC-10 we could take on fuel as well as offload it. This required me as a KC-10 aircraft commander to maneuver within 12 feet of a tanker, going hundreds of miles per hour, and maintain a stable platform while connected to the tanker via a telescopic refueling boom. Since the KC-10 is a very large aircraft and develops a great deal of inertia when maneuvering or accelerating, it required me to master some very precise flying skills to perform receiver air refueling safely. As an aircraft commander in training, this was an important part of my training.

For me to become a fully qualified receiver pilot meant I needed to be able to stay connected with a tanker in almost all situations: day or night, cloudy or sunny, dry or rainy, smooth or bumpy, etc. I needed to train in different conditions to ensure that when the time came, I'd be able to complete any mission the Air Force asked me to perform. Of course, there were limited visibility and severe weather conditions where we wouldn't even attempt a refueling because it was too dangerous. In the "rather die than look bad" (RDTLB) KC-10 community, though, we considered calling off a refueling a last resort.

Near the end of my training, I needed to qualify in night refueling. My first night training mission called for flying across northern Texas to New Mexico and rendezvousing with a KC-135 in an airwork area for refueling training (an airwork area is airspace set aside specifically for military flight training). That night promised to be particularly challenging, because the KC-135s were on restriction. They were not allowed to use their autopilot for refueling that night, since there had been equipment problems recently. This problem was mostly apparent when they refueled jumbo aircraft like the KC-10. To us, this meant the tanker platform would be less stable than usual, especially since our refueling would take place in a confined area where we needed to conduct quite a few turns. This made staying connected with the KC-135's refueling boom even more problematic. On top of all this, the weather briefing called for thunderstorms and associated turbulence near the refueling area. It looked to be a difficult night, even before we took off.

By the time we made radio contact with our KC-135, an hour after takeoff, the weather had deteriorated. Thunderstorms were now just outside the refueling area and were causing turbulence and intermittent thick clouds in the area. In fact, they considered the northeast quadrant of the area unusable, so would need to maneuver even more to stay within the area's boundaries.

We entered the area and saw the lights of the KC-135 in the distance as we conducted our rendezvous. Our tanker rolled out one mile in front and one thousand feet above us, just as planned. It was also turbulent, as we expected. When we climbed to within one-half mile of the KC-135, we entered a thick cloud bank, losing sight of the tanker.

Regulations required us to stop closure with the tanker if we can't see it within one-half mile of contact. As I was pulling the throttles back to maintain position, Major Bill Poggi, my instructor, directed me to continue. I cited the restriction on closing within one-half mile without having positive visual contact with the tanker. He told me he understood, and I should continue, slowly closing with the KC-135.

Major Poggi was near-legendary in the Air Force KC-10 community. He was the chief of all aircrew training at Barksdale and he had more KC-10 flying experience than anyone on base. He was revered as being just an exceptionally good pilot and a very capable instructor. So I continued my closure. Slowly.

We broke out of the clouds within a quarter-mile of the tanker. I continued closing and then stabilized the plane in the pre-contact position before inching forward for the final few feet prior to making a physical connection with the KC-135 refueling boom. At this point, we were in significant turbulence, with both planes being buffeted by the thunderstorms near the area. As we went in and out of the thick clouds, we alternated between having the full moon light up our tanker, merely feet in front of us, and losing sight of it completely.

It was crazy. I continued my closure towards the KC-135, constantly making the slightest of movements with the throttles and the aircraft controls. I remember thinking, *Why the hell is he letting me continue this?* and *Surely, he must know how dangerous this is!* Yet, as reluctant and scared as I was, I sure as hell wasn't going to back down in front of this revered pilot. RDTLB.

We remained on "Mr. Toad's Wild Ride" for well over 20 minutes, even though the weather never cleared, and the turbulence remained. Major Poggi even made me disconnect and close-to-contact several more times during our little adventure. By the time we finished, I soaked my t-shirt with sweat from the stress of the evening. I've never had to focus so intensely for such an extended period as I did that night. I felt the slightest mistake on my part would have endangered me and my crew. After the refueling was complete, we returned to Barksdale, did several practice approaches and landings, and called it a night.

The next day, we gathered in the mission planning room to prepare for the following day's training mission — my second night refueling. And I discovered we were going back to the same area with another KC-135. We received a preliminary weather briefing and, once again, the forecast was for thunderstorms near the refueling area. Holy crap. No way in hell did I want to go through that again. Yet, I continued planning the mission. Far, far worse than finding myself unable to refuel the night of the flight was backing down from a mission ahead of time simply because of a weather forecast.

That following day, before driving to the squadron, I remember pulling out my Last Will and Testament from my files and putting it on the desk in my living room in my apartment. I didn't expect to not come back, but I was still somewhat unnerved by what had happened the previous night. I didn't feel 100 percent sure, under the same (or worse) conditions, things would turn out well.

As it happened, the weather was much better, and the training flight was far less stressful. I came to find out later I developed something of a reputation because of that earlier flight. The other crewmembers on my flight were impressed with my poise, presence of mind, and flying skill under those difficult circumstances. This helped get me off to a great start in my new squadron.

So, other than showing how crazy I am, what did I learn from this situation? First, I discovered how much ability I have. While it's always good to be cautious while flying, it could have been just as much of a problem if I had underestimated my abilities. By pushing myself up to and beyond what I believed were my limits, I proved to myself I could handle much more than I thought I could.

Confidence in my flying skills was useful as I continued my Air Force career. Sometimes I just had to get the mission done, even under some very difficult conditions. These challenges included nighttime deliveries of supplies to Marines on an unlit airfield in Somalia, mid-ocean air refueling over the Atlantic at night in bad weather, and landing at minimum visibility during a snowstorm in Germany, just to name a few.

Later, when I upgraded to KC-10 instructor pilot, I learned several techniques on how to remain safe while teaching a student how to takeoff, land, and air refuel. I discovered that Major Poggi, by gently "guarding" the throttles and control yoke, was more in control than I understood that night. I also saw how he let me push my limits, so I could discover how capable I was. And for that, I have an even deeper appreciation of what an outstanding instructor pilot he was. Thank you, Major Poggi, and all the other flying instructors and leadership mentors I've had in my life, for helping me believe in my own abilities.

Chapter 9

Hate Mail

*Me addressing the assembled 19th Air Refueling Group
in the theater.*

Courage can be much more than physical bravery. In the fall of 1999, I was a newly promoted colonel and Air Mobility Command had recently given me the privilege of commanding the 19th Air Refueling Group at Robins AFB, in Georgia. The 19th is one of the Air Force's most historic units and can trace its distinguished record back to the 19th Bombardment Group, one of the 15 original combat air groups formed by the Army before World War II.

The group's spirit was legendary. We were known as the Black Knights. The group was very proud of our identification and our motto was "Checkmate to Aggression," dating to the early days of the Cold War. The local community also regarded the Black Knights well — it awarded us the annual Warner Robins Community Service Award in 2000 while I was commander. I felt deeply honored to command this amazing KC-135 group, with its 500+ dedicated airmen organized into four squadrons.

My new job had quite a few challenges, though, even from the beginning. One of these was having to take over from perhaps the one person in the Air Force I didn't get along with. My predecessor and I had a history going back many years when he and I were in the same KC-10 squadron at Seymour Johnson AFB in North Carolina. My experience with him showed him to be an arrogant bully with a lack of integrity. Before my arrival at Robins, he spread the word throughout the 19th they would be very disappointed in me. He told them they should be sorry to see him leave because they would surely dislike me.

Apart from the obvious lack of professional courtesy this showed, it was also a blatant attempt to set me up for failure by making him look good by comparison. While it irritated me that I had to deal with these undertones as I was taking command of a new group, none of it surprised me. I ignored this nonsense, both publicly and privately, until several months after taking command. That's when I received an anonymous letter in my official mailbox.

This is odd, I thought. The letter only had my name written across the front. No address or return address. I opened it and started reading. I was shocked. The two-page, typewritten letter was full of insults, curses, and accusations, all directed at me in the most personal, degrading terms. The letter asserted I was a terrible commander, I was working people too hard, and I had better shape up or I was going to completely lose the respect of the entire group. The letter alleged the author was the leader of a large group of airmen in my unit who felt I was failing miserably as a commander and I "needed to change before it was too late." After that closing threat, the unsigned letter ended. I knew I needed to address these accusations — I couldn't let it go.

Part of the reason it shocked me was I didn't think I had been in charge long enough for anyone to form this strong of a negative opinion about me. More importantly, I found it hard to believe someone would be so bold as to send the group commander a threatening letter like this, wherein the writer supposedly spoke for a large group of people who felt the same way.

Apart from being a blow to my ego, it was a direct attempt to undermine my confidence as a commander, and I resented it. I had a staff meeting with my deputy and four squadron commanders scheduled for the next day. At the meeting, I distributed copies of the letter and asked them if they knew anything about it or if they knew of any people in their units who felt this way. I could tell they were embarrassed to even be dealing with this situation. They all professed to not know anything about this, which I'm sure was true. They also advised me to toss the "crank" letter and forget about it. I thanked them for their recommendations and adjourned the meeting.

I slept on it that night. The letter still bothered me when I woke up the next morning. It upset me someone or a group of people under my command felt so disconnected that it compelled them to compose and send me such an offensive, threatening letter. It also caused me to think about what I had done or hadn't done to help create this situation. I wondered what I could do to resolve this and prevent something like this from happening again. I decided on a course of action.

The next day, I met with my commanders and told them what I intended to do. At our monthly commander's call in two days, I planned on standing up in front of the entire group and discussing the situation. I wanted to make a slide presentation of the letter and address the issues line-by-line. I would then talk to the group about changes I would make to increase my visibility and availability. I wanted the airmen of my group to have more access to me to discuss any issues that concerned them.

My commanders were aghast. They argued against what I intended to do. They said by highlighting this letter, I was giving the author more credit and visibility than he or she deserved. They were afraid it would backfire on me. We were all still getting to know each other, and I sensed they were worried I might not be able to pull it off. They were unanimous in their opinions. The only one of my leadership team who dissented wasn't present at the meeting. My Senior Enlisted Advisor, Chief Master Sergeant Garry

Frost, told me later he thought it was a fantastic idea for me to address the issue head-on. While I had decided to do just that by the time I talked with Chief Frost, I very much appreciated his vote of confidence in me.

I didn't dismiss my commanders' fears lightly, though. Each of them was an accomplished professional, and I respected their judgment. During my career, I witnessed commanders and other leaders who embarrassed themselves and undercut their authority and reputation by reacting strangely to difficult circumstances. While none of this ever led to disobedience or anything that extreme, it was a terrible situation for them to be in. I remember feeling sorry for them. Good Lord, that would be the worst of all outcomes — I shuddered thinking about that possibility.

Was I letting my ego get the better of my judgment? Were my commanders right — were they perceiving something I was not seeing? I still had almost two years left in command. The absolute last thing I wanted to do was shoot myself in the foot because of wounded pride. I didn't want to be "that guy." Despite my concerns and questions, I went ahead with my plan. I felt I needed to trust my judgment. I needed to show some spine to the men and women under my command by facing this issue head on.

When the time came at the Commander's Call for my presentation, I stood up on stage in front of the theater full of hundreds of airmen. I told them I had received an anonymous letter I wanted to discuss with them. I then asked for my first slide. I specifically instructed my executive officers to include everything in the letter — don't edit and don't censor. The initial slide was full of curses, accusations, and foul language directed personally at me. The already quiet theater went dead silent. Nobody wanted to make a sound or even move. They waited for my reaction. Once I was sure they had read the slide, I looked directly at them and spoke up clearly in a strong voice.

"I know what you're all thinking. You're wondering why my mother would be writing me at work" (slight emphasis on the last two words).

After a split-second pause to absorb what I had just said, the theater burst into laughter. This broke the ice. They saw I didn't want to chew them out, nor did I intend to plead with them to treat me nicely. I was there to talk to them like adults.

I then described why each of the accusations the writer made, slide by slide, line by line, was incorrect or resulted from a misunderstanding. I explained that I took responsibility for this letter as I hadn't been as connected with them as much as I should have been. I then told them how, in addition to blocking time specifically for them to see me throughout the week, I was immediately instituting a walk-around program where I would be informally coming to one of the four squadrons for an unscheduled visit at least one day per week — this way I would see each squadron on a monthly basis. I also invited the individual(s) who wrote this letter to please come see me, so we could discuss their concerns.

The feedback I received from my Commander's Call briefing was enormously positive. I believe it completely changed the group dynamic. From that point on, the group was fully behind me. They gave me the benefit of the doubt when I asked them to face our many challenges and operational demands over the next two years. This incident also inspired me to have greater personal contact with the men and women in my group, which was a positive result for all of us. To close the loop, the author(s) of the anonymous letter never showed themselves to me or any of my commanders. I wasn't surprised. I expect they went radio silent from that point on, since I never heard another word about this subject.

After my talk, one of my bright young captains took the time to seek me out and tell me how inspirational my talk was. He even compared my reaction to this letter with what Abraham Lincoln might have done — the captain was reading "Lincoln on Leadership." I wasn't sure how to react, so I smiled and said, "Complimenting the boss, eh? I can tell you'll go far." Inside, though, I was flattered.

While the examples I've described in this first section of my book show the importance of courage and belief in myself, this message applies to every one of us. I'm grateful I lived to first learn this lesson in pilot training and was able to apply it throughout my Air Force career. I use this fundamental truth up to this day. After I completed the one-year pilot training course, my father, mother, and younger brother Kevin made the trip to Reese AFB to watch me graduate in a formal ceremony in December 1978. My father, standing tall in his brigadier general's uniform, came up on stage and presented me with my silver Air Force pilot wings. It remains one of the proudest moments of my life.

PART 2

COMPASSION

*Group photo of our wonderful, compassionate San Diego friends
from a 2016 birthday party. I'm in the back row near the middle.
My wife JoAnn is in the back row on the far left.*

Chapter 10

Broken Boundaries

Picture of me at Christmas in 1967.
I was in 7th Grade and had just turned 13.

I was 13. I felt sick to my stomach. My drunken mother had not only crossed the line, she had obliterated it. I didn't know what to do, and I was scared. I would have given anything and everything to be anywhere else. Of the countless upsetting incidents associated with my mother's alcoholism, there is one that stands out as the worst — worse than all the rest put together.

My father was out of town on a business trip, which was often when my Mom would have her drinking bouts. One night, my mother came into my room and asked if I could go with her. She had been drinking. I felt a knot in my stomach. I got up, even though I was in my pajamas, and followed her into her room. She asked if I could stay with her for a while. My mother, when she had been drinking, would often feel very lonely and sorry for herself. In hindsight, she must have suffered from depression and the alcohol just magnified everything. Regardless of the causes, this all felt terrible. I was frightened. I didn't know what to do. It felt so damned creepy.

She asked if I could lie down with her, just to keep her company. I did, even though everything in me felt awful. It's painful just writing this, almost 50 years after it happened. She asked me to snuggle with her, like my father does, kind of spooning with me behind her. We lay there for maybe 10 minutes at the most. I never have been so horribly uncomfortable in my life. I wished I could be anywhere else in the world. Anywhere else.

I was terrified of what she might ask me to do next; although my thoughts didn't focus on anything specific. Finally, my mother said I could leave. I got up as quickly as I could and went straight back to my room. I think she realized how intensely and painfully uncomfortable I was. She also must have realized how very inappropriately she was behaving. I don't believe she ever intended anything beyond physical touch and comfort because she was lonely and depressed. Frankly, I don't care why she did it. She should never, ever in a million years exposed me to that situation. She should have known better, alcohol be damned.

Dealing with the memory of having an alcoholic parent requires facing some painful truths. Otherwise, the shame and fear of things that happened years ago just continues to grow, affecting all aspects of life. If I could take the memory of that night out of my mind, I would in a heartbeat. As it is, I have had to come to grips with what happened and be at peace with it. I was angry with her, and it's okay for me to have been angry.

I believe in my heart she never intended to hurt me because she was a loving soul throughout her entire life. That was her essence, and it showed through whenever she wasn't drinking. I know, too, I did nothing to cause this. I know for me to be at peace I have to let go of the anger. Holding onto it only continues to let it fester and eat at me from within. By shining a light on what happened without guilt and shame, I am releasing this from my life. Be gone and good riddance.

Several years before, I sat in front of my father in our backyard. I was 10-years-old, and I was in tears. Mom had just chewed me out again, and it made no sense. I was old enough to understand she had been drinking. When she drank, she was so angry and hurtful, and her behavior wounded me and my siblings. "Please do something, Dad," I implored him. I wanted him to make her stop.

Instead, he calmly explained my mother had a chemical imbalance. That's the reason she acted the way she did. He said some of her brothers and sisters had an alcohol problem, too. As he spoke, the message I heard from him was that there was nothing he could do. We could only hope it gets better. And, for God's sake, don't talk about it with anyone, especially someone outside of the family. We don't want people to know about your Mom's problem, because it will reflect badly upon us as a family. Even at age 10, it seemed hopeless.

To help put my childhood in context, I'd like to describe my four wonderful siblings: three brothers and one sister. The oldest of the five children in our family is my brother, David Cornell Hurd. Born five years ahead of me, Dave has a bigger-than-life personality. A graduate of the University of California at Berkeley like me, he is a very successful country swing band leader (The Cornell Hurd Band), with quite a following in Austin, Texas. He is also the father of two cherished adult sons. No one has a bigger heart or is more generous than Dave — the enormous number of friends he has in Austin and throughout the music community is a real testament to that. After the death of our parents, Dave has made a huge effort to keep in touch with all of us. He has always been an extremely supportive big brother.

My sister Caroline Hurd is three years older than I. She also is very compassionate, and it shows — she always makes us feel welcome when we visit. Caroline skipped a grade in elementary school, which turned out to be a real indication of her dedication and work ethic, as she suffers from dyslexia, a serious learning disability that went undiagnosed for years.

She earned a bachelor's degree in radio and television from San Diego State University and a master's degree in systems management from the University of Denver. Caroline and her husband Marc Ricketts married in 1989 and they have a kind and talented son Colin. She recently retired from Lockheed Martin where she worked more than 40 years in Quality Control and Product Assurance — the same company and career field where my father was so successful.

My brother Drew Hurd is one year and nine months older than I am — he was two grades ahead of me growing up. Drew is one of the brightest and most well-informed people I know. He also had the strength to choose a different path than the rest of us: Drew was the one who decided to not graduate from college. Instead, he followed his passions and own interests, which typically involved studying birds, being out in nature, and learning more about the Bay Area. He and his wife Lucie have been married since 1978. He recently retired, as well.

My younger brother Kevin is two years behind me. While all of us boys were athletic — we were all on the same recreation league softball team while I was in college — Kevin was by far the most gifted and dedicated athlete. He was a good baseball player, but his real strengths were football and track/field. Kevin (nicknamed "Bubba") was a standout defensive lineman for Homestead High School and received recognition for his excellence by being named as one of the best nose guards in the Santa Clara Valley Athletic League his senior year. He also was a superb shot putter and discus thrower in high school and went on to compete at De Anza Community College as a freshman and sophomore. With my encouragement, Kevin joined the Air Force after graduating from Cal Poly San Luis Obispo and became an RC-135/KC-135 navigator. He retired in 2014 as a lieutenant colonel after a very successful career in the Air Force Reserve. Kevin also earned a master's degree from Embry-Riddle University while working full time as a reservist. Kevin and his wife Doris have been married since 1989 and they have two beautiful daughters. Their older daughter, Christine, was a high-school valedictorian and graduated from Harvard with a degree in political science. Their younger daughter,

Cathy, is a sweet and severely disabled angel who has inspired Christine to pursue medical school.

Even though there were only seven years between the youngest and oldest, each of us had to deal with our mother's alcoholism separately. We were close with each other, but discussing our mother's alcoholic behavior was off limits. Mom was wonderful when she was sober, which created a huge disconnect. We loved her dearly and wanted the "consistent, loving, supportive" Mom to be present, yet, the "irrational, blaming, embarrassing" Mom would show up at the most inopportune times. We could never tell when Mom would be drinking, so there was a constant, underlying, day-to-day fear associated with her erratic behavior.

As adults, we have talked little about Mom's alcoholism. Even now, with many years gone by and both of our parents deceased, it's still difficult for us to discuss the issue. It also apparently didn't affect the older children as much as it did the younger ones. Dave (the oldest), has said he didn't notice Mom's alcoholic behavior that much. He, of all of us, has had the most direct experience with substance abuse, as he went through rehabilitation 30 years ago for cocaine addiction and has remained sober ever since. His wife also had a serious alcohol problem, which was a leading contributor to their divorce years ago. He knows intimately what addiction looks like and the severe problems it can cause, so I take him at his word on this.

Yet, I recall the many Thanksgiving dinners where we boys would bet when (not if) Caroline would get so angry with Mom she would storm out of the kitchen — it seemed to happen every year. Holidays were a trigger for my mother's drinking. While it would be irrational and unfair to blame all our problems on her drinking, I can point to behaviors in me and my siblings linked to having an alcoholic parent: addictions, feeling victimized, overeating, fear of confrontation, passive-aggressive behavior, hoarding, and the list goes on. All of us don't have all these behaviors, but I can point to each one of these in at least one of us. We all had to deal with these urges in some manner — even to the point of deciding to go in the opposite direction.

As a child, as time went on my fear of embarrassment became pronounced. What if my friends were to see my mother when she's drunk? What will they think? What will they say to the other kids? I can't let this happen. I can't take any chances. I've got to be sure we do things at my friend's houses, not mine. If someone's picking me up in their car, I've got to look out the window and meet them out front, before they can come to the door.

It was a life that had an underlying fear and dishonesty even though everything else was going great. I hate the impact my mother's alcoholism had on my life as a child, a teenager, and even as a young adult. My mother drank for as long as I can remember. The first time I remember a drinking problem was that day when I was 10 and I talked with my Dad. Before that, I recall anxiety and confusion regarding my mother's behavior. Which way do I go? What do I do? It was a feeling of helplessness, of feeling responsible for something I had no control over, of feeling that I had to make the situation better, but not knowing what to do.

Throughout the years my mother was drinking, how I wish my father would have realized this was never going to get better and he, as the responsible, sober adult, was going to need to do something to directly address the problem. I wanted him to stand up to her, to protect us from her verbal abuse. But he didn't. I think part of the problem was that Dad didn't drink at all, so he didn't really understand the attraction and the effects of alcohol, much less the problem of alcohol addiction.

He was also an engineer. He looked at things from a scientific, analytic perspective and he was very good at that. We were all proud of Dad's achievements in quality control: he was elected president of the American Society for Quality Control (now known as ASQ) in 1977-1978 and had annual awards and a foundation named after him — they were all dedicated to recognizing international excellence in executive leadership. They also elected him president of the Flight Safety Foundation.

Apart from being extraordinarily accomplished and distinguished, Dad was just a wonderful man and a loving father. Yet, when confronted with the data point of "Scandinavian people have a hereditary susceptibility to alcoholism," it was his rigorous, objective, fact-based engineering background that shut his mind down to other possibilities. My mother was of Swedish descent. Her siblings had alcohol problems. Therefore, my mother had alcohol issues because she is genetically disposed towards that. It was a scientific fact. End of discussion.

My mother and I had a complicated relationship. Her battle with alcoholism and its effect on me is a thread throughout this book. There's much to unpack. There's also a great deal of love and light around her and I want to show that side of her, too. As with my father, I also eulogized my mother at her funeral in 2002. I've included that as Appendix D.

Chapter 11

Shame

Sign in front of Grant Elementary School, Los Altos, California

I stood in front of my much admired, beloved sixth-grade teacher. I didn't know what to do or say. My face burned red and my head spun. Ashamed, hurt, and confused, I couldn't think straight. Mr. Smith (not his real name) called me "sick." He called me "twisted." He said I should be ashamed of myself. He directed his anger full force at me. I felt paralyzed. I couldn't do anything but stand there and just listen to him as he went on and on and on. I wanted to be somewhere else, anywhere other than right there, right then in front of him as he shamed me. I used all my focus and energy to stop myself from crying. I couldn't even begin to absorb what he told me because I was so confused. I didn't expect this, and it felt horrible. But here was Mr. Smith, telling me I should be ashamed, so I must have done something terrible to deserve this. Why did this happen? I didn't know. It made no sense.

It was the fall of 1966, I was 11-years-old, and I was running for a school-wide office in the annual election at Grant Elementary School. Grant School was a neighborhood suburban K-6 school built in the 1950s. It was a response to the need to teach all the baby-boom children. I had gone there since kindergarten, and I wanted to become the Boys Activity Manager. I had asked Mr. Smith to be my sponsor. I felt I was popular enough to get elected, but I didn't want to compete with the "really popular" classmates of mine who would run for class president and vice president.

Mr. Smith was my teacher in sixth grade at a time when few male teachers taught in elementary school. He was young, he was cool, and the boys in my class thought he was the greatest thing ever. We all wanted to hang around with him. We all emulated him. My friend Mike Doyle and I even signed up to take extra schoolwork on Saturdays — a special class where Mr. Smith taught us geology and took us on field trips to rock formations in the local area. It was fun.

Because Mr. Smith was my favorite teacher ever, I asked him to be my sponsor as I ran for election. All of us who were candidates required a faculty sponsor. Part of his duties as sponsor required him to approve any speeches I would make. I had come to him that afternoon after school to get my speech blessed before I gave it to the entire school in a week. I expected getting his approval would be easy as I showed him what I wrote.

In 1966, the Vietnam War had already been going on for years and our U.S. commitment to the war was ramping up. I was an 11-year-old boy who was very much into strategy board games where famous battles and military campaigns would be refought between players. I spent hours and hours with my friend Mike and other friends of ours refighting the D-Day invasion, the battle of Waterloo, Rommel's Campaign in Africa, and the like. My focus, like many boys my age, was on heroism and struggle and victory.

The speech I wrote reflected this mindset. I'm sure my speech was over the top. I remember it involved several of my friends pillow fighting with each other in front of me while I was on stage giving my speech. I think it also involved encouraging other boys to play strategy games, too, probably in a tournament of some type. I don't remember any other specifics. I'm sure that's a result of the negative feelings I have surrounding this event. What I do remember in great detail is Mr. Smith's reaction to my speech.

When I gave my ideas to Mr. Smith, he just sat there silently. And then he exploded. His face grew red, and he raged at me. He called me sick and twisted and told me I should be ashamed of myself. I remember walking home after Mr. Smith's tirade. I was in a fog. I think my friend Mike was there with me, but I'm not sure. I remember telling him about what happened either that day or the next. I was so damned embarrassed. I didn't know how to describe it. When I got home, I told Mom. I told Dad after he got home from work. They were aghast in their own, very reserved, Midwestern way. They wanted to talk to Mr. Smith. I said please don't. I just wanted the whole thing to go away, and I didn't want to make a bigger deal of this than it already was. I wanted no one else to know about this and I was afraid if Mom and Dad confronted Mr. Smith, things would escalate and everyone would find out. They respected my wishes. I also told them I wasn't going back to Mr. Smith's Saturday geology class. They understood and didn't even try to convince me otherwise. I'm so glad they didn't.

That weekend, my father spent an entire afternoon with me. As there were five children in our family, it was rare to have Dad all to myself. He made a very special, very pointed speech to me that day. He told me there was absolutely nothing wrong with me. He said he and Mom knew I was a wonderful young man and they didn't doubt me "one iota." I didn't know what an iota was, but I understood what he was trying to tell me, and I loved him for it.

Mr. Smith said nothing further about our meeting. He never talked with me about my dropping out of his Saturday class. I don't remember anything about giving an election speech or being the Boys Activity Manager, but I received a certificate saying thanks for doing the job. I must have written a far more conventional sixth-grader speech and been elected. Mr. Smith never apologized for what he did. I know I would recall that.

What causes an adult teacher to lash out like he did that day? What overcame him with anger so great he took it out, full force, on an 11-year-old boy? And not just any boy, but one who clearly admired him and was a good, respectful student. It still makes me angry to think about it, even to this day. He had no right to behave like he did. And to just let it sit there and not to apologize is unbelievable.

His lack of regret confirmed in my 11-year-old mind that he really thought I deserved all those hateful things he said. He was the adult — he should have never addressed me in that manner or tone. He needed to show maturity and guide me to a more appropriate way of expressing myself since he felt that was necessary. He never should have pulled the crap he did.

Being 50 years removed from the event, several things are clearer now. First, and this is no excuse for what he did, I'm sure he must have been affected, maybe even threatened, by what was going on in Vietnam. I remember some teachers were hurrying up to get married because married men were getting deferments from the draft. He never expressed his views on Vietnam, but it may have been he was angry about the war and I came along at the wrong time, representing something he was afraid of, or opposed to, or both. And he exploded. I can understand the urge to react the way he did, but he never should have expressed his feelings like that. I have wondered if he even knew or cared about the effect his anger had on me that day and how it has affected me throughout my life.

So how did this affect me? I can tell you I've engaged in direct one-on-one, in-your-face win/lose confrontation as something of a last resort. Whether this reluctance resulted from my painful experience with Mr. Smith, my mother's alcoholic behavior, or some other combination of factors, I don't know. What I can say is I developed a keen ability to collaborate and negotiate with others. Throughout my career, I've often led people to creating solutions to problems thought to be intractable.

There were other times when I needed to put my foot down and stand firm when I felt standards and discipline were lacking. Those occasions were infrequent. That "my way or the highway" approach can work in the short term and may even be necessary in an urgent situation, but the demanding, dictatorial style of leadership is toxic to everyone involved. Perhaps, in a way, Mr. Smith helped guide me to the leadership style that has served me so well. Regardless, it doesn't change the fact his behavior toward me was completely inappropriate.

Chapter 12

Freedom of Religion

Article I of the Constitution protects our right to freedom of religion.
(debate.org)

I wasn't sure how to react to what Lieutenant Colonel Benson was telling me. An academy-educated lieutenant in his squadron, a pilot, had just refused to wear the required Air Force flight uniform for her flight the next day. This young officer attended a local Pentecostal church near Robins Air Force Base and the elders of the church convinced her that wearing a flight suit or even the standard Air Force camouflage-patterned battle dress uniform (BDUs) was against God's word. Their guidance came from a passage in the bible they interpreted as directing men only to dress as men and women only to dress as women. To the church elders that meant the lieutenant should not wear pants. And she was prepared to accept any disciplinary actions that came her way.

As her group commander, I needed to decide how to approach this situation. I never heard of anything like this before. The lieutenant was a good officer and pilot, and the Air Force had invested a lot of money in her. Yet I was the commander of a military flying unit and we had safety and operational standards all of us needed to adhere to. And I knew the potential for this to blow up into a national news story was high. There had to be a way to resolve this that was fair to everyone involved — the lieutenant, my group, and the Air Force. We needed to find it.

Mr. Smith's outburst toward me when I was in sixth grade also taught me the painful, degrading effect of shaming another person. I don't know how aware I was of this before I turned 11, but I certainly knew about it after that. I believe I've been successful largely because of my supportive, considerate way of engaging with others.

One of the greatest compliments I ever received was at my going-away dinner at Robins AFB when my group command was complete. During my two-year tour, the hard-working and talented men and women of my 19th Air Refueling Group (19 ARG) won two consecutive Air Force Outstanding Unit Awards and a host of other unit and individual recognitions for superior performance. Most prominent among these awards was the naming of the 99th Air Refueling Squadron, the premier KC-135 flying unit in my group, as the recipient of the Carl Spaatz Trophy for being the best air refueling squadron in the entire Air Force for the third consecutive year. Winning this Air Force-level award three times in a row had never happened before or since and it reflected directly on the wonderful, dedicated officers and airmen in that squadron.

During presentations at my going-away dinner, Lieutenant Colonel Scott Reese, the outstanding commander of the 99th, presented me with a gift on behalf of his squadron and said to the assembled audience "Colonel Hurd is proof nice guys finish first." I could not have been given a more heartfelt, wonderful compliment. It meant I succeeded in leading my men and women in the way I wanted to.

I also have long recognized that public shaming and bullying behavior is a trigger point for me. I've witnessed this behavior in the Air Force and

I've called it out when I see it. I will not tolerate it. On one occasion, when I was 19 ARG commander, one of my maintenance squadron commanders publicly made fun of a senior noncommissioned officer who had a stuttering problem. This happened when the sergeant gave a presentation while my deputy was running a staff meeting and I was away from base. When I returned, my deputy told me about the incident and I couldn't believe it. I called the squadron commander in my office and I asked him point blank, "What the hell is your problem?" Things went downhill from there. There were other issues with his squadron, too. I eventually ended up firing this commander for cause, resulting in him having to retire abruptly because the Air Force passed him over for promotion to lieutenant colonel, which is a story I address later in this book (Chapter 23 "Bad Decisions").

I also made a point of giving the senior master sergeant who he ridiculed a unit-funded trip to attend a Tuskegee Airmen conference. The Tuskegee Airmen were the heroic black World War II aviators who were many of the most courageous and highly decorated American fighter pilots fighting the Nazis in Europe. They accomplished this extraordinary record despite fighting institutionalized racism in the U.S. It was a huge treat for us to send the sergeant to this event. More important than that, it was a great recognition for the outstanding work he was doing in the group.

I still remember the big smile on his face when I offered the trip to him. It was almost as big as the smile he had when he told me about the three-day event after he returned home. Even though money hadn't been allocated for this trip, I worked with my financial people to shift funds to make it happen. By sending the sergeant to this conference, besides rewarding his great work, I wanted to send a message to everyone else in my group that I wouldn't tolerate anyone, regardless of rank or position, degrading another group member while I was in command.

Compassion can also take the form of respecting the rights of an individual even if his or her behavior/decisions are in direct conflict with Air Force policy. During my first year as 19th Air Refueling Group commander, I was confronted with the first lieutenant KC-135 copilot who refused to wear her Air Force flight suit.

We came to find out no one had ever come up against this in the history of the Air Force or any of the other military services. The first thing the lieutenant's squadron commander and I needed to do was decide how we wanted to approach this situation. One possible response was to force the issue by ordering the young pilot to change into her flight suit and fly her scheduled training mission. By refusing a direct order, she would have been subject to military discipline, resulting in an end to her career and a possible less-than-honorable discharge.

Even though we would have been justified to go in that direction, I didn't want the needless punishment and loss of a promising young pilot because we were impatient. We needed time to come up with a solution, so we replaced her on the flying schedule and directed her to go home until further notice. Throughout this, I was fortunate to have a very capable officer, Lieutenant Colonel Bryan Benson, as her squadron commander. We worked well together to resolve this.

After ordering the lieutenant to go home for now, I raised the issue to my three-star boss, the 21st Air Force commander at McGuire Air Force Base in New Jersey. From there, it quickly went up the chain of command to Air Force headquarters at the Pentagon. Because this issue involved freedom of religion, a basic American right, the Department of Defense decided a panel of senior military religious leaders and legal experts would need to study it. They would determine whether the lieutenant had a legitimate claim and if the Air Force should make any accommodations for her. Because of the slow-moving nature of headquarters decision-making and the widespread consequences of any conclusions (this issue impacted all the military services, not just the Air Force), it was obvious early on this would take months to decide.

In the meantime, what do we do with the lieutenant until they decide her case? I gathered with my squadron commanders and gave them direction. We needed to put the lieutenant to work in an administrative capacity where she could perform duties in her blue uniform combination with a skirt, typically used for office work. Even though none of us believed she was trying to get out of working, it was important to show she wasn't getting a free ride during this time. I impressed upon everyone in the group the lieutenant was to be respected and treated like the officer she was. I gave direction that we would reprimand anyone caught harassing the lieutenant. I would not tolerate disrespectful or inappropriate behavior. My four commanders understood and passed the word to the men and women in their units.

During the months of back-and-forth between me, my bosses, and the legal and religious experts at headquarters, the issue rose in prominence. At one point, the story was such a big deal that Peter Jennings covered it on the ABC Nightly News national broadcast. Meanwhile, the lieutenant performed her assigned duties professionally and with a good attitude. Finally, Air Force headquarters handed down a decision. They determined wearing a flight suit or BDUs was not against religious beliefs. The lieutenant would have to comply with Air Force policy or face military punishment. We informed her of the decision. At the same time, we placed the lieutenant on the ground training schedule. We scheduled her to attend an emergency procedures class with other crew members. The class started promptly at 0800 the next day. She would need to wear her flight suit.

We knew the lieutenant would talk with her church elders, since she had been doing a great deal of that throughout the previous six months. We also expected they would try to talk her into maintaining her resistance to wearing pants. Despite the lengthy decision process at the Pentagon, we still didn't know how the lieutenant would react. We made it a point to not put any pressure on her. Still, we would get indications of what she was thinking. Some days, it seemed she was leaning one way and some days the other. Finally, 0800 came around. The lieutenant showed up to her training appointment in her flightsuit. She informed her commander and her immediate supervisor she was still having difficulty deciding and she might come to a different conclusion after talking with church elders that evening.

At the end of a long day, the lieutenant walked into her commander's office and told him her decision: she would continue to participate in all Air Force activities, even though it required her to wear a flightsuit. The deciding factor for her was how warmly the squadron welcomed her back after her absence. She was clearly very moved by how wonderful people were to her despite the "problems" she had caused. We were all glad to have her back.

The lieutenant was only one young and low-ranking officer in my organization that numbered more than 500 members. Was it worth the effort to give her an exception to policy for all those months? I would give an unequivocal "yes" as an answer. By showing compassion and respect for the lieutenant's religious views, even though most of us saw her perspective as rather extreme, we showed to the entire group the Air Force is a humane and respectful organization. Individual views count. When there is conflict, a process exists to determine what is appropriate given the laws of this country and the needs of the Air Force.

On a personal note, I believe the lieutenant very much appreciated the treatment we provided her. While I haven't followed her progress in the Air Force, she was an excellent officer and pilot at the time — highly regarded in all respects. I was also touched she made a point of being present at my going-away dinner at the end of my tour as commander — senior officers and NCOs are usually the ones who attend those events. I'm glad we approached her situation with as much sensitivity and compassion as we did. I'm also very proud of the wonderful men and women of my group who responded so magnificently during the months-long appeal process, and especially when the lieutenant returned to flying duty.

Chapter 13

Straighten Up and Fly Right

I am accepting the 1995 Air Force Maintenance Effectiveness Award on behalf of my squadron, the 6th Air Refueling Squadron, at March Air Force Base in California. Presenting the award to my squadron is the 722d Air Refueling Wing Commander, Colonel Richard Mentemeyer.

After nearly crashing my T-38 that October night in 1978, I finally had gained barely enough speed to start a slow, careful climb. I carefully pulled back on the control stick, trying to maintain minimum airspeed while moving away from the ground. I was at a 45-degree angle to the runway, since I had stopped turning my T-38 so I could regain every bit of life-giving airspeed. I was now aimed directly at the other planes on the parking ramp. I crossed the edge of the airfield at perhaps 10 feet above runway altitude. My jet screamed over the parked aircraft, then the hangars next to the airfield, and then over base housing as I climbed straight ahead.

I didn't pull the throttles out of afterburner or make any turns until I reached pattern altitude and leveled off. Heart pounding, breathing heavily, and adrenaline flowing throughout my body, I knew I had just barely escaped dying. I hadn't had time to even absorb that until that moment. I had been completely focused on reacting to the threatening situation. Now the full impact of the near-disaster hit me like a ton of bricks.

It was at that point the air traffic controller called me on the radio: "Rees 31 Solo, what are your intentions?" The whole episode from start to finish had taken less than a minute. What I intended to do next was the last thing on my mind. I was just relieved to be alive. As I sped along at 180 miles an hour, I realized I needed to make a very important decision.

Fast forward to the middle of 1994. It had been over fifteen years after my near-fatal experience at pilot training, and the Air Force had recently promoted me to lieutenant colonel. I had just taken command of the 6th Air Refueling Squadron, a KC-10 tanker unit at March Air Force Base in California. This was very much the pinnacle of my career up to that point — I was now in charge of 200 dedicated officers and airmen who flew and maintained the McDonnell Douglas KC-10. The 6th was one of two flying squadrons, along with my old unit (the 9th Air Refueling Squadron), in the 722d Air Refueling Wing at March. Commanding the 6 ARS was an inspiring, humbling, amazing assignment.

The only disappointing aspect was that my assignment would be shorter than the usual squadron command. I would only have 13 months in the position because March was closing as an active duty Air Force base due to post-Cold War congressional Base Realignment and Closure (BRAC) decisions. My job was to ensure the squadron continued to fully meet its robust operational commitments while getting the unit ready to move to its new home at Travis Air Force Base in northern California.

When I took command in mid-June 1994, I immediately noticed some significant performance and attitude issues with the men and women in the squadron. I sensed a general feeling they believed the other squadron (the 9th) received more than its share of the credit for the great work the wing was doing. I also noticed the officers under my command seemed hesitant to make decisions. I sensed this was because they didn't believe leadership fully supported them in their roles as aircraft commanders and flight commanders. A persistent "victim" mentality also appeared in the quality and timeliness of paperwork crossing my desk, especially as it pertained to officer and airman performance reports.

None of this was acceptable. Because I didn't see any imminent safety issues, I chose to wait at least a month before making any drastic personnel changes. That way, I could make a fair determination who were my top performers and who were unsuited for their positions because they lacked training or were failing in their leadership roles. Right around the one-month point into my command, things came to a head when Colonel Lorenz (the wing commander) pulled me aside and told me he had just walked unannounced into my squadron maintenance building.

Rather than calling the building to attention and approaching the wing commander to see what he wanted, my airmen "scattered like cockroaches" (the colonel's words) into their offices. Apart from being embarrassed, this behavior from my men and women confirmed my squadron was on the wrong track. I assured Colonel Lorenz I would address the issue with my airmen.

Sometimes, the most compassionate thing a leader can do is to let people know, in no uncertain terms, that they are failing, and they need to immediately straighten up and fly right. Anything less than that is doing them a severe disservice. After finishing my discussion with the wing commander (or rather, when he had finished with me), I returned to my squadron and told my first sergeant to let every officer and non-commissioned officer in a leadership role know there was a mandatory meeting in the squadron briefing room the next morning at 0800. Only performing scheduled flying duties would be an acceptable excuse for not attending.

At precisely 0800 the next day, I had my first sergeant call the officers and NCOs to attention as I walked into the briefing room. Under normal circumstances, I would then tell my squadron to take their seats and I would begin our meeting. On this occasion, I kept them at attention for the entire time — standing tall, eyes forward, arms straight down by their sides. After

I arrived at the front of the room, I turned and spoke to them in a clear, direct voice.

"This is a one-way communication. I will talk. You will listen."

I told them what the wing commander had said. I told them the squadron had a crappy attitude, and I wasn't going to stand for it. Performance reports coming across my desk were late and of poor quality and we were failing the men and women who expected us to lead them. I told them I expect every officer and NCO to be a leader — no excuses. Aircraft commanders, whether at home station or deployed elsewhere, were the final decision-makers and I would hold them responsible for the performance of their crews. Those serving under the officers will obey direction they have been given without complaint.

"What I am saying is not negotiable — this is how things will be done from now on. Period. I am not a loser and I will not accept loser attitudes in my squadron. Get used to it and shape up."

Immediately after I finished, I paused for a second to let what I said sink in, and then I walked directly out of the briefing room. I did not dismiss the men and women in the room as I normally would — I had directed the first sergeant to let them know when I left the building, so they could return to their duties. I wanted my squadron leaders to get the full impact of what I was telling them — and they did. I made a point, however, of not mentioning anyone by name. I felt there was no need to single any individuals out to shame.

The squadron got the message. I only needed to make a few key changes in the leadership structure of the unit, replacing a few underperforming officers and NCOs with others whom I felt were more capable and energetic. I reinforced established processes and started tracking performance reports, providing personal feedback from me on every report down to the lowest-ranking airman. I also gathered my aircraft commanders to re-emphasize the importance of their crew leadership and how I was holding them responsible for mission success and their crew's behavior while away from home station.

I am very proud to say the men and women of the 6th responded extremely well. Over the next year, our squadron won the Air Force Maintenance Effectiveness Award, recognizing us as being the best large aircraft maintenance unit in the entire Air Force. The wing commander also nominated us for the best air refueling squadron in the Air Force. I was very pleased to see such amazing progress and I believe my "kick in the pants" helped the men and women get back on the right track. From that point on, they performed superbly — they needed a little course correction, that was all.

After six months in command of the 6th, I deployed to Al Dhafra Air Base in the United Arab Emirates (UAE) to lead the 4413th Expeditionary Air Refueling Squadron, a unit of 250 airmen from throughout the Air Force, mainly consisting of aircrew and maintainers from the two KC-10 squadrons at March. The purpose of our deployment was to provide mid-air refueling support for fighter and airborne control aircraft over the no-fly zone in southern Iraq (Saddam Hussein was still very much in power).

The name of the ongoing mission was Operation Southern Watch and by that point it had been operating 24 hours a day since shortly after the 1991 Gulf War. There was no end in sight to our commitment. This was my second Southern Watch deployment to Al Dhafra — I had a previous tour in 1993 when I was the 344th Air Refueling Squadron Operations Officer (the 344th, another KC-10 unit, was based at Seymour Johnson Air Force Base in North Carolina).

Near the end of our lengthy deployment to Al Dhafra, a master sergeant in my squadron opened his gear locker one morning to discover a big yellow stripe painted on the back of his flightsuit. This vandalism appeared to be intended to shame the sergeant because he wasn't behaving "like one of the guys." This sergeant, an excellent flight engineer, was quite reserved and didn't participate in many of the enlisted crewmember off-duty activities while we were away. When I found out about this, I was appalled. Nobody was going to undermine the self-confidence of my men or women, regardless of rank or position.

Compassion can also take the form of standing up to bullying. I needed to make a point to everyone in the squadron that I would not tolerate this behavior. In response, I did something unusual. I contacted my group commander back at March, halfway around the world and 12 time zones away, and told him what had happened. More importantly, I told him what I intended to do about it. He supported me completely, which I very much appreciated. I then gathered my deployed operations officer and all six aircraft commanders together — these were the seven ranking aircrew officers I had with me during the deployment. I told them I was cancelling the contractor cleaning crews for the latrines until further notice. The mostly Filipino and Pakistani cleaning crews would still get paid, but they would be taking time off.

Instead, each aircrew would take turns cleaning the bathrooms until the individual or individuals who had vandalized the sergeant's flightsuit came forward and admitted their actions. The aircrews would come in and perform the cleaning on their scheduled days off. I directed the operations officer (my second-in-command) to draft the schedule and make it happen starting the next day.

I also talked with my officers about why I was doing this. I told them it was our responsibility to support the dignity of every airman in my squadron and a breech like this was unacceptable. Everyone in the unit, aircrew or not, needed to understand the importance of this. I also told them I expected their full support, and they needed to communicate this same message when they were talking to their crews.

I'm sure my aircraft commanders weren't looking forward to doing this, as they would clean toilets along with their copilots and enlisted crewmembers, but I never received any pushback on any of it. I believe they understood and supported what I was doing and why I was doing it. I also think they knew I had made up my mind and there was no way I would change it.

This exercise only lasted about a week because we were redeploying back to our home base — our tour was over after many months of being away. I never got the name of the individual(s) who painted the yellow stripe on the sergeant's flight suit, but I never expected to. That wasn't the point. My goal was to impress upon my airmen that bullying and shaming anyone was not acceptable behavior in my squadron and in my Air Force. I'm sure I got the message across. I expect the person who vandalized the sergeant's uniform either kept his mouth shut or, if someone knew him, he received a lot of grief for what he did.

Good.

Chapter 14

Don't Ask, Don't Tell

Deployed Airmen in front of KC-10 at Al Dhafra Air Base, UAE.
(U.S. Air Force)

Early in my 1994-95 deployment to the UAE, I received a written complaint from an airman first class in my security police detachment. It was unusual to get a written complaint to begin with. An airman typically comes to a supervisor or commander and raises the problem verbally. The complaint I received alleged my executive officer, a young captain, was sexually harassing this airman by making unwanted advances in her personal quarters.

The reason the airman went to the length of making this a formal, written complaint was because she was making it against an officer. She was frustrated because she had already told the previous commander, who had done nothing about the problem before he redeployed and I took over. The harassment claim was also complicated by the fact that both the officer and

84

airman were women. Furthermore, there were racial overtones, as the officer was black and the airman was white. This situation had all the hot buttons.

Life in the military is very different from civilian life. The intersection between work, social, and family life is far greater in the military. As an officer, the people I worked with were the people I socialized with. Often, our children and spouses were friends. When I deployed, the people I worked, socialized, and lived with were exclusively military. It was total immersion.

This was good in terms of reinforcing our friendships and promoting squadron cohesion. It could also create numerous strains. We were all away from our families for many months. Deployments placed significant stress on everyone, both military members and families back home. As you might imagine, we didn't necessarily get along with everyone we deployed with.

Long hours at work for months on end could strain even the best of friendships, much less test our relationships with people with whom we may not have been too compatible beforehand. Serious problems sometimes developed that would never have occurred under more routine circumstances. As the commander, I insured my squadron performed well and my people were treated fairly. I also had wide latitude to deal with issues, including some strict disciplinary options if I needed them.

Because I was a lieutenant colonel squadron commander, the biggest hammer I had was the Uniform Code of Military Justice Article 15 ("Article 15" for short). Under an Article 15 punishment, I could take away pay, reduce an airman in rank, or even imprison an airman for a short period if the infraction was severe enough.

As a unit commander, I considered issuing an Article 15 only in the most severe circumstances. For an officer, an Article 15 was a complete career ender — there was just no recovery from that. Even receiving a simple letter of counselling would lead to non-promotion and an early termination of an officer's career.

In 1994, the status of gays and lesbians in the military was complicated. The year prior, the Joint Chiefs of Staff had done a thorough review and delivered a recommendation to President Clinton that homosexuality was incompatible with military life. Yet, society's perspective was changing, and the rules associated with discharge from the military because of homosexual behavior changed along with that.

The result was the "don't ask, don't tell" policy, whereby commanders couldn't ask about the sexual orientation of a military member and the military individual was not required to tell their supervisors about their sexual orientation. Despite this change, the policy still stated that an airman "having sexual relations or displaying romantic overtures with members of the same sex or telling anyone about their sexual orientation is considered homosexual conduct and is a basis for involuntary discharge."

Being discharged in this manner was devastating emotionally. The stigma resulting from an involuntary discharge could also remain with a person well beyond military service and affect his or her ability to gain follow-on employment as a civilian. In my opinion, "don't ask, don't tell" was highly unfair, since it committed gay and lesbian military members to keeping their personal lives secret for fear of being found out.

Despite the continued negative repercussions, it was better than the previous policy, which required the Air Force Office of Special Investigations to actively search for homosexuals in the military, intending to discover and discharge them. A couple of times early in my career, I remember squadron friends just disappearing. One day we were joking around at work and the next they were gone from the squadron and the Air Force. No forwarding address or phone number. No explanation given, although we knew what probably had happened because of the way things were handled. It was terrible. To this day, I feel bad for them. I didn't even have time to say goodbye or offer words of support, it all happened so quickly.

As an officer, and especially as a squadron commander, I was responsible for upholding the regulations, policies, and orders of those officers senior to me. I could not pick which ones I would enforce and which I would ignore — uneven implementation of rules was one of the surest ways to lose credibility and undermine discipline. This meant I had to enforce the official policy regarding discharge of service members who were gay or lesbian. End of discussion.

Still, I could provide different levels of attention to specific regulations without being disobedient. Of the many priorities I had to focus on as a commander, discharging gays and lesbians was at the absolute bottom of my priority list. And it never, ever moved up.

When confronted with the sexual harassment complaint against my executive officer, I immediately recognized it as a major issue that had far-reaching consequences for the individuals involved. Because it was a written complaint, I needed to respond in writing. I couldn't deal with it by simply conducting a counseling session and issuing a verbal reprimand. Since it was a second occurrence due to inaction from the previous commander, it required a substantive response from me.

I also knew that anything I did would get back to the captain's home unit (she was not from March Air Force Base), resulting in her having a near-zero chance of promotion and potentially causing her to receive a less-than-honorable discharge, with huge, negative, post-Air Force repercussions. Here was a young woman who had volunteered to serve her country as a military officer and was facing life-altering consequences based on a policy I believed was unfair.

Yet, the policy had been reviewed and approved by the Chairman of the Joint Chiefs of Staff with the knowledge and concurrence of the President of the United States. I needed to find a solution that wouldn't violate policy yet would be fair to both my executive officer and the airman who filed the complaint. I needed to be creative, and I needed to be compassionate.

The day I received the complaint, I called the nearest Air Force lawyer, who happened to be forward deployed to Saudi Arabia. I described what I intended to do. I wanted to be sure my plan didn't violate policy or regulations even if it was unorthodox. After a lengthy discussion, he deferred to my judgment as the commander on the ground. He also confirmed I was not doing anything illegal or against regulations. That's all I needed to hear. I asked him to prepare the appropriate documents and send them electronically, which he and his staff did promptly.

Later the next day, I called my executive officer and my first sergeant into my office. I had asked my first sergeant, a female Air Force master sergeant, to be present for my discussion with the captain. I wanted someone from my command section to witness the conversation in the event the verbal orders I gave were called into question later. Additionally, even though the first sergeant was enlisted, and the captain was an officer, I wanted an older, more mature woman available, so the captain could have someone to talk to afterward if she needed.

I began our meeting by describing why I had called her (my executive officer) into my office and presented her with a copy of the official complaint. I continued with a summary of what the airman said, including a description of the behavior that made her feel so uncomfortable. I could see the blood draining from the captain's face. She was terrified and confused. She knew what this might mean, and she was scared.

When I finished with the specifics of the complaint and any other pertinent unwritten details, I paused. I did that only to make it clear the introductory portion of this meeting was over. I wasn't going to give the captain a chance to speak yet. In the confusion and fear of the moment, I did not want her to say anything she might regret later. I continued:

"Let me tell you what I think happened. I think this was a misinterpretation. I think you were being overly friendly, and the airman may have misunderstood your intentions. Because you didn't recognize her reaction, you also didn't pick up on any of the cues she sent that your perceived advances were unwelcome. Am I correct?"

I was giving her an "out" and she jumped at it like a drowning woman would grab a life preserver.

"Yes, sir. That's exactly what must have happened. I'm so sorry. I didn't mean to come across that way."

I then pulled a letter out from my desk.

"Captain, this is a letter of counselling for unprofessional behavior signed by me. I'm giving you a direct order, in front of the first sergeant, to not have any contact with the airman who filed the complaint for the rest of the time you are deployed. This includes both at work and in quarters. If you need to contact the airman, you go through the first sergeant or me. No exceptions.

"I'm placing this letter in my upper desk drawer, where it will stay until you depart here in one month when your tour is over. If you haven't violated my order by the time you leave, I will tear up this letter. There will be no record of our discussion.

"If the airman informs me you've had contact with her outside of the guidelines I've given, that will tell me you do not understand the gravity of the situation you're in. It will also indicate you are incapable of following a direct order from your commanding officer. In that event, I will send this letter to your squadron commander at your home base and it will go in your officer performance records. Do you understand?"

"Yes, sir."

I'm sure the captain also knew I would be within my rights to consider Article 15 punishment for disobeying a direct order, depending on how serious the infraction was. She knew even without an Article 15, all of this could end her career.

"Do you have any questions?"

"No, sir."

"If you would like to talk with the first sergeant about what just happened, she's available. You're dismissed."

The captain stood at attention and saluted. "Yes, sir." I returned her salute, she did an about face, and she and the first sergeant left my office.

I knew the captain was shaken by this whole experience. I also knew she realized she had dodged a bullet. I had no doubt she would comply fully with my orders and she would be on her way home a month from now, her deployment completed with her Southwest Asia Service Medal pinned proudly to her uniform.

My next step was to talk with the airman first class to let her know I had acted upon her complaint. I called the airman into my office, along with the first sergeant. I told her I had written a letter of counselling for the captain and was holding it in abeyance until the conclusion of her deployment.

I described how I had given the captain a direct order to cease any contact with her for the rest of her deployment. If the captain violated the order, I would send the letter of counselling to the captain's commander and her military career would likely be over. I asked the airman if she had any questions about what I had done.

"No, sir."

Did she believe any other actions on my part needed to take place?

"No, sir."

I think I might have scared the airman, too. She may not have realized that by filing a formal complaint, she had set a series of actions in motion. I don't believe the airman ever wanted to harm the captain's career. She only wanted the captain to back off. This entire experience may have been a lesson to the airman, too: a lesson in her own power. I hope it also showed to her the Air Force and I took her sexual harassment complaint seriously, despite the neglect that occurred when she made her original accusation.

Both the captain and the airman successfully completed their tours in the UAE without further incident. I checked in with the airman occasionally before she deployed back home to ensure everything was okay. She assured me it was.

While all of us would have preferred not to have had to deal with this situation at all, I'd like to think the captain and the airman both appreciated how it was handled. While it took a couple more decades until gays and lesbians could serve openly in the military, I hope on this one occasion I gave a young captain a second chance, while showing a young airman the Air Force cared about her well-being.

Were my reactions to the situations I described in this part of my book, and others like these throughout my adult life, a result of my sixth-grade teacher's bullying behavior towards me? I suspect the answer is at least partially yes. In that way, I should thank him for helping inspire me to behave in a way that is supportive and morally defensible. And, after 50 years, I can accept that and recognize the value I received, even as repugnant as my experience with him was.

I still believe his behavior is indefensible. Meanwhile, I also appreciate what he unintentionally taught me — the importance of treating others with respect and compassion. I learned this lesson well, and it has served me throughout my life, helping to make me the successful officer I became.

PART 3

INTEGRITY

My parents came to Nebraska to visit my brother Kevin and me at Offutt Air Force Base, Nebraska in early 1988, and we made a point of taking this picture. It's the only photo we have of the three of us in our Air Force uniforms. I had just been promoted to major and Kevin had recently become a captain. Dad had been a retired brigadier general for nearly 20 years.

Chapter 15

Continuing Concern

The front gate at KI Sawyer Air Force Base, Michigan.
(KI Sawyer Heritage Air Museum)

The phone rang in the living room at the house my roommates and I were renting off campus. I walked over and picked up the receiver.

"Hello."

The instant my mother spoke, my heart sank to my feet. I had an awful feeling in the pit of my stomach. She was giddy and slurry and drunk. I realized she would never be better. And I felt like I couldn't do a damn thing about it.

My father's conclusion that Mom's drinking was inevitable and there was nothing we could do continued until the middle of my college years.

Mom's alcoholism had gotten so bad by that point even my father couldn't reason it away. With his insistence, she checked in to a residential medical facility for alcohol rehabilitation ("rehab") in 1975. I should add "for the first time," since it wouldn't be the last.

Based on her resistance to rehab and her resentment toward my father for "making her go," I'm sure the effort was doomed from the start. Yet we didn't know at the time and all of us prayed this was going to "cure her." She would be sober. The craziness would end, and Mom would be our loving, reliable Mom all the time. Or so we hoped.

About a month after she had gotten out of rehab, Mom called me at the house I was renting with two of my friends at college. I'll never forget that day and the hopelessness in my soul to hear her drunken voice on the other end of the phone. After one month of sobriety, she was drunk again. Damn it.

Despite Mom going to rehab, my family still wasn't talking about her alcoholism. Even trying to approach my brothers and sister was fruitless. We all knew what was going on, although I think at least one of my siblings was in denial. We didn't want to talk about it. It was too painful to deal with, even amongst ourselves. So, we went about our own business, hid the pain, and ignored the situation as best we could.

For years, my mother continued to be a problem drinker. I was afraid she would show up drunk at important events, like my officer commissioning ceremony, my graduation from pilot training, or even my wedding. Thankfully, Dad knew when he should watch Mom extra carefully. I believe Mom even realized being drunk at some special events in our lives would be unforgiveable. She didn't want to go back to rehab, so she kept herself in check, somehow, during those times. Still, it was unnerving. The uncertainty was there — an underlying fear my mother might be drunk at some meaningful occasions in my life, coloring all our memories with her embarrassing behavior.

My Mom's drinking was a presence in my life for many years after my childhood. Sometimes it affected me directly in the Air Force even though I lived far from home. On one occasion, Dad and Mom came to visit me at KI

Sawyer AFB in the Upper Peninsula of Michigan, just south of Marquette. This was early during my first assignment after pilot training — even before I met my first wife, Carol. We had a good time and there were no obvious problems while they were there. However, after they left, the angry manager of the billeting office confronted me. There were small bottles of alcohol missing from the Distinguished Visitor Quarters where Mom and Dad were staying.

The billeting manager wanted to know who damn well would pay for the missing bottles. I knew at once what must have happened. I'm sure Dad had tried to control Mom by not allowing her to drink while they were in Michigan. But Mom just took the bottles, drank, and did as she wanted to. The manager demanded payment, or he was "going to press charges." I told him I was sorry this happened, and it must have been an oversight by my parents. I offered to pay the bill. He accepted my check, but then lectured me about how wrong this was and how he could press charges, how he had to go out of his way to track me down, etc., etc. He was still going on and on when I cut him off.

"Look," I said. "I paid you. There's nothing more I can do. This meeting is over."

And then I turned around and walked away. I didn't care if he had finished or not. It felt good to just shut him up and leave him standing there.

Chapter 16

Carol

KC-135A doing a water-injected takeoff. This was the aircraft I flew at KI Sawyer Air Force Base in Upper Michigan on my first assignment. The "A" model had small, underpowered engines and required water injection to increase air density during heavyweight takeoffs. "Wet" takeoffs also created a lot of smoke. The newer engines are much better. (U.S. Air Force)

I sat there stunned and dumbfounded. It was early in 1983. Carol, my wife of less than two years was talking, and I couldn't believe what she was telling me. It was noon, and we were in a public restaurant in Colorado on a ski trip with Carol's sister Janet and her husband. We had planned the trip for a long time, but in recent months Carol had been treating me like something the cat dragged in. Angry but controlled, I had just expressed my alarm about how she had been behaving toward me.

We had an opportunity to be "alone" at the restaurant (without family or any other distractions), so I decided it was as good a time as any to confront her with it. After I described how she had been treating me and how terrible it felt, I asked her for an explanation. What did she want to tell me? Did she even realize how she behaved toward me?

Faced with what I said, all she could muster was a very impassive, "I know I've been a bitch toward you." No apologies. No remorse. Nothing else to add.

"What? Why?" I asked. My head was spinning. Carol's lack of feeling took me aback. It made no sense.

She then launched into a rehearsed, monotone description of how she was tired of being known as Captain Bruce Hurd's wife and she wanted to have an identity of her own. She wanted to move to Nevada and start a life there. It took a while before I could even muster a response.

"What the hell?!" I responded. "We've only been married two years. You want to move to Nevada?!" This discussion was going from very bad to much worse. I expected none of this. And I couldn't wrap my head around why it was happening . . .

Carol and I met in early 1980 in the remote Upper Peninsula of Michigan when the Air Force stationed me at KI Sawyer Air Force Base. I was a KC-135 copilot on my first operational Air Force assignment after pilot training. From there, we moved to March Air Force Base in Southern California in late 1982. I had landed a premier assignment to fly the KC-10 tanker, the Air Force's newest plane, fresh off the assembly lines.

Carol always expressed her desire to leave the Midwest and our move to California excited her. The first thing we did was buy a brand-new home in a nice suburban neighborhood. The change in her attitude months later was both unexpected and unexplainable. I didn't understand why she would feel this way. I told her if we needed to go to counseling to work on this, I wanted to do that, but her moving away to another state just wasn't acceptable.

"What caused this?" I asked. She couldn't give me an answer. She only said it was how she felt, and she didn't want to explain it. Frustrated and confused, I asked if she understood how she was acting toward me. Would she at least treat me better?

"Yes, I know. I've been treating you badly."

Her response was unemotional, almost numb.

"I'm not going to change."

The conversation had devolved to where I was at my wit's end. Not knowing what else to do, I gave Carol an ultimatum. Either she could change her attitude and at least agree to go to counseling after we returned home, or I would file for divorce. I told her she needed to agree by the time our vacation ended in two days.

I felt I had no other option, no other leverage than to throw the one card I had left to play that might get her attention. I couldn't see how I could live this way, with her either treating me like crap or moving away. I'm not sure which would have been worse, but neither was acceptable.

Carol hadn't been looking at me this entire time. She was staring past me or off to the side. After I delivered my take-it-or-leave-it offer, Carol looked up and we locked eyes.

"I'm not changing."

I met Carol at a squadron party in January 1980. She was friends with the wife of one of my pilot friends in the 46th Air Refueling Squadron, our KC-135 unit at KI Sawyer. Since I was about the only single copilot in the squadron, I'm 99 percent sure my friend Bob and his wife Sandy invited Carol to the party to meet me. Even if our meeting wasn't by design, the attraction between the two of us was instantaneous. Carol was beautiful, with long, blonde hair and a very attractive face. More than that, she was funny and intelligent and had a radiant personality. She made it very clear she was interested in a relationship, and I jumped at the opportunity. We started dating each other exclusively the next week.

After completing KC-135 qualification training and survival school, I arrived at KI Sawyer and the 46 ARS in June 1979. I became mission-qualified once I finished local area orientation, completed a battery of additional training courses, and certified on our nuclear support mission. The entire process took about two months. Training courses revolved around things like handgun qualification and chemical defense training. Chem defense training included going through a tear-gas detonation in the "gas chamber" — the intent was for us to develop confidence in our gas masks.

The lengthiest and most intense part of my mission qualification was preparing for and going through Single Integrated Operational Plan (SIOP) certification. The SIOP was the massive strike plan the U.S. military would execute in the event nuclear bombs or missiles struck us from the Soviet Union. Air-to-air refueling of nuclear-armed B-52 bombers was a critical part of the SIOP, and certification involved intense academic study and a great deal of memorization. For me to qualify as a mission-ready copilot, I had to learn everything from my SIOP-related flying procedures to the intricacies of decoding classified messages.

Under normal circumstances, the squadron would wait for an entire four-person crew to arrive on base before sending them through SIOP certification. That way, each of the individual crewmembers could share the responsibility for learning the material and master their part before being called upon to face the formal certification board led by a colonel in the 410th Bombardment Wing (410 BMW), our parent unit at Sawyer. Newer crewmembers could also benefit from having more experienced officers go through this with them.

Because we were so short of copilots in the 46 ARS, the squadron sent me through the entire process by myself, even though I was brand-new and would go through this alone. I had to learn everyone's part, including the aircraft commander's, the navigator's, and the boom operator's responsibilities. I studied hard and practiced my presentation at night and on weekends. I didn't think anything about having to learn everyone else's role, figuring this was normal. But it wasn't at all.

Colonel Rodriguez, the wing's deputy commander for operations, led the four-member certification board. He and the rest of the officers on the board, including my squadron commander, listened as I gave my half-hour presentation, followed by 30 more minutes of detailed questions and answers. Once we finished, they pronounced me mission-ready on the spot.

I was excited. I wasn't a student or in training for the first time in my life. It felt amazing and empowering and I reveled in my new freedom. I was now a full-fledged member of the 46th and the "real" Air Force. I knew I still had a lot to learn. After many years, though, I wasn't in training mode any longer. I was a 24-year-old pilot/officer/bachelor, and I was excited to embrace my new life.

What I found was I spent a lot of time "pulling alert." I was placed on alert duty within days after being certified as mission-ready. Our mission in the 410 BMW was to conduct nuclear war. All our training revolved around that. The wing had six B-52 bombers loaded with nuclear weapons on 24-hour alert, 365 days a year. Each bomber had a mated KC-135 tanker from the 46 ARS topped off with fuel. My crew's job was to conduct air refueling over the Arctic Circle so our paired B-52 could reach its targets in the Soviet Union. Each bomber had six crew members, and each tanker had four.

All 60 of us (24 tanker crewmembers and 36 bomber crewmembers) stayed for a week at a time, three or four to a room, in an alert facility next to the ramp where our fully loaded aircraft were parked. The secure facility was guarded by a dozen or more armed security police and surrounded by barbed wire with entrapment areas leading to the building entrance. Our twelve aircraft were cocked and ready to launch. Alert crews were required to takeoff within minutes of receiving notification. The squadron scheduled crews for one week out of three on alert and we did our flying training during the two weeks we weren't on alert.

In the fall of 1979, the 46th had five copilots depart to join commercial airlines. The squadron only had 21 assigned copilots to begin with and someone had to fill those six lines of alert. That meant me. I was the most junior copilot in the squadron and I was single, so it wasn't as if I even had a wife and family at home. As the fall began, I found myself scheduled for back-to-back alert tours, only being pulled off to get an occasional takeoff and landing to ensure I had flying currency. Then I went back on alert.

It wasn't long before I realized this was a pattern, and for the foreseeable future, alert would be my life for every two weeks out of three. I had a choice: do I complain about the situation or do I continue to do the best job I can and keep a good attitude? Of course, I chose the latter. The absolute last thing I wanted was to get a reputation as an attitude case. Besides, people in the squadron soon appreciated me, if only because my presence on alert meant they might not have to pull extra tours. And because I didn't whine about my situation.

My near constant alert duty, though, killed any social life I might have had otherwise. Meeting women was difficult to begin with because there are few people who live in the Upper Peninsula. The local communities in the UP, while friendly to the military, pretty much kept to themselves. I'm sure they said the same thing about us — military people can be insular, too. To top it all off, I found the large majority of officers in my squadron and on base were married, so there weren't many single guys to hang with and meet other people. It was also unusual for spouses of my squadron-mates to know any single women, since the base was far away from even the few non-Air Force people living in the UP.

For me, meeting someone as beautiful and charming as Carol was a dream come true. After a few months, our dating became serious and Carol moved her things from her parents' home in Illinois to an apartment in Marquette, about 20 miles from base. She had been living with her sister Janet while she worked at a local hospital as a registered nurse. Carol and I dated through the year and I proposed right after I came home from a six-week deployment to Europe and Saudi Arabia just before Christmas, 1980. We married in May 1981 in a military ceremony at the base chapel, complete with crossed swords and everything. I felt like it all was going my way... I loved my new wife and how my life was turning out.

Later in 1981, I went through KC-135 aircraft commander training. This was a huge and very exciting step for me, as I now had my own crew and was pilot-in-command of the missions I flew. It was only three months after my upgrade to KC-135 aircraft commander in February 1982 that Strategic Air Command chose me to fly the KC-10. The selection took me somewhat by surprise since I knew the competition was extreme — almost everyone wanted to be a part of this new and exciting opportunity. On my selection board, I found out later, there were only six pilots chosen out of 600 who applied.

The KC-10 tanker, a military version of the long-range McDonnell Douglas DC-10 jumbo jet, was the newest aircraft in the Air Force inventory. It was big and beautiful, and we all wanted to fly it. One of the biggest attractions of the KC-10 was it didn't pull alert like the KC-135. In talking with my assignments officer, I also found I would be assigned to March Air Force Base near Riverside, California to help start the brand new 9th Air Refueling Squadron. It was all perfect. This was a once-a-career opportunity. Carol was completely on board, too, as we both eagerly looked forward to moving away from the isolation and the freezing winters of the Upper Peninsula and toward the excitement, warmth, and opportunities of Southern California. Plus, I would be closer to my parents, brothers, and sister. It was thrilling and wonderful. Everything was coming together in the best possible way.

Chapter 17

Difficult Decision

Facing a difficult decision in 1983. (pixaby.com)

We arrived home after our 1983 skiing vacation and Carol hadn't changed her mind — she still wanted to move to Nevada by herself and start a life there. We landed at Ontario Airport on Friday night and I told her she needed to go someplace else for the weekend — stay with a friend or something. I didn't want her around our house.

Nothing Carol did surprised me by that point, so it didn't upset me when she cheerfully agreed to turn around, take her bag, and leave for three days. I was actually relieved I wouldn't have to deal with her. It would just be me and our two cats alone at home that weekend. I needed time to think.

I visited Mom and Dad that Sunday to have dinner — we had arranged it before Carol and I went on vacation. My parents lived just two hours away in Tarzana, California in the San Fernando Valley near Los Angeles. When I arrived at their townhouse, I made an excuse about why Carol wasn't with me that night. I dreaded telling them about what was going on. My parents were married for 42 years by then and, like many couples their age, they were devoted to each other. My two older brothers were both married and no one in my parents' families had ever divorced, except one uncle and one aunt.

I was afraid Mom and Dad would try to talk me out of what I was planning to do. There had been no trouble between Carol and me. Just five months earlier, Carol and I were staying with them on weekends as we waited for our house near Riverside to go through the inspection and closing process before we purchased it. There were no problems between the two of us then. All was well. And now this. What would they think? What were they going to say? Would they be disappointed in me? I had a knot in my stomach.

After dinner, I carefully approached the subject with them. Mom and Dad stopped what they were doing and paid close attention, not saying a word. They knew I was upset by how I started the conversation, and I'm sure they also knew they should just let me talk.

I calmly, but deliberately, told them all about Carol's recent behavior. I spoke in measured words and tone — I didn't want to get visibly upset while describing what was happening. I closed by telling them about my ultimatum; that Carol, knowing I would file for divorce, said okay and left for the weekend. Once I finished, they paused before responding to make sure I was done with what I needed to say. They then responded in a very supportive and loving way.

In their own understated Midwestern manner, my parents let me know they supported me completely and whatever I decided, either file for divorce or stay with the marriage, they were behind me 100 percent. They said they knew me, and they knew what kind of man I was, and they would do whatever I needed them to do to help me. I told them I felt I could handle this, and I appreciated their love and support more than I could say.

True to their word, they never interfered with what transpired over the next year. They didn't overtly take sides because they wanted this to be my decision without interjecting their expectations. Yet I knew I could count on them, no matter what. I thank God I was so fortunate to have them as parents.

The next day, a Monday, I found a lawyer from the Riverside legal referral directory in the phone book and went to visit him. I felt dazed and numb. Carol had made no attempt to contact me since she left Friday night. I didn't even know where she was or how to get hold of her if I wanted to. It was clear she hadn't reconsidered her stance.

I felt almost as if I were sleepwalking. I was going through the motions for something I couldn't believe I was doing and I didn't want to happen. This was the first of many times during my divorce when I found it hard to wrap my head around all the pain and hurt and shame I was going through. It often seemed surreal. I frequently had to disconnect myself emotionally just to function. The whole situation felt terrible.

The lawyer did his due diligence, getting to know me and my situation and asking me if I considered a separation rather than going straight to a divorce. I told him I had, and this is the way I wanted to proceed. When I saw Carol again on Monday evening, I didn't even ask where she had gone. While she was surprised I had filed for divorce like I had threatened, it didn't upset her at all. She even remarked, "I didn't think you had the guts to go through with it." I'm not sure why she would even make that statement, regardless of what she believed, but it certainly didn't help the situation.

Her distant attitude continued until, several weeks after my filing, Carol became extremely remorseful. As if a switch had flipped, her behavior instantly changed from night to day. She was so, so sorry, she said. She realized what a mistake she made, and she wanted my forgiveness.

"What the hell was happening now?" I wondered. I asked her point-blank what caused this sudden change of heart. Carol explained she now understood the consequences of her behavior. She was sorry, and she wanted things to go back the way they were.

While life wasn't as tense after Carol "came to her senses," the fact remained I didn't trust her, and I had no real idea why her attitude had reversed. In hindsight, I expect anyone looking at this situation from the outside would have seen it for what it was.

Just a couple weeks following Carol's change of heart, her long-time best friend, Michelle, and Carol's sister Janet, came to stay with us while they attended a nursing conference nearby. Michelle and Janet were registered nurses, just like Carol. One Saturday, while Carol was at work and they were at home with me, I asked Michelle and Janet what was going on with my wife. Janet was familiar with the situation since we stayed with her and her husband during that terrible ski trip in Colorado.

It wasn't too long before Michelle spoke up. She didn't want to be a part of Carol's excuses any more. Carol had used Michelle as a reason she had to leave home on at least one occasion. Michelle explained it wasn't true. Carol never saw her. Instead, Carol was having an affair with one of her hospital patients, a man named John. Carol had been using Michelle and other friends as an excuse for meeting with John.

The reason for Carol's abrupt turn around in attitude was that she told John I had filed for divorce. The two of them could now be together. Much to Carol's surprise, John didn't want that, so he broke it off with her. Carol realized she had really screwed things up, and now she was about to be without either a boyfriend or a husband. Janet, who had been just as confused as I was regarding Carol's behavior, was furious with her sister.

I was both grateful and angry after talking with Michelle. I was grateful I now knew the truth. I was angry and stunned, betrayed by the woman I loved. This was the woman whom I promised to love until death do we part. And she made the same promise to me. Now it was plain her vow meant nothing to her.

She discarded me like yesterday's trash when she thought she had a better deal, only to come running back when her better deal turned out to be a mirage. And worst of all, she destroyed my trust in her. She not only had the affair, which was horrible by itself, she lied and manipulated me every step of the way. She maneuvered me so perfectly, I was the one who filed for divorce. That way, she could be free of me and nobody would blame her when she reemerged with John somewhere down the line.

I felt like someone had kicked me in the gut. I didn't know what to believe or whom to trust. When I found out the truth, I went into self-protect mode. I had been around Carol long enough to know she was irresponsible with money and I worried she would run up all our joint credit cards in an act of desperation because I was "cutting her off."

To Carol, getting a new credit card was the same as receiving the card's credit limit as cash in her checking account. She saw only the need to address the minimum payment for each card every month and we had more than a dozen credit accounts, each with thousands of dollars in credit limits. She never worried about paying them off — that was my job, since I handled the family finances.

So, the first thing I did was cancel all our jointly owned cards. Because the world was so much less connected than it is today, their cancellation wouldn't create a major upheaval in our lives, just an inconvenience. That night, Carol approached me to make love. She was a beautiful, sexy woman. When I told her I wasn't interested, she began to lecture me about how we would never get back together if I didn't even try.

It was then I told her I knew about John and I knew she had been lying and manipulating me for months. She claimed ignorance. She said I was mistaken, it wasn't like that at all. I stopped her in mid-sentence. I told her it was Michelle who told me the truth. And her sister knew, too, because she was there when it came out. Oh, and don't try to use any of our joint credit cards anymore because I cancelled them all.

Carol was silent. I could tell she was trying to figure out a way to deny this, to spin the story so she wasn't guilty. That it hadn't happened at all. That it wasn't true. But she couldn't. Caught in a series of lies and deception, she couldn't explain her way out of the problem she created. So, perhaps for the first time in her life, Carol was being held accountable for her actions.

While I took no joy in what was happening, there was relief. I finally knew what was going on. After months of confusion and worry, I could regain control of my life. I had taken back my future. It wouldn't be until a year from then, when the divorce was final and the property had been divided, that I truly felt I could look beyond what was happening in the next day or week or month.

Just getting through the divorce was painful. Carol and I lived in the same house the entire time. We didn't make enough to own a house in Southern California and maintain a separate residence nearby. Carol continued trying to get us back together. She enlisted work friends of hers to come over and talk to me about how she had a change of heart and I should reconsider the divorce and forgive her. Meanwhile, my mother's drinking continued, causing entirely different problems . . .

"Squadron scheduling. This is Captain Hurd," I answered the phone. It was the middle of another busy day and I was at my scheduler's desk at March Air Force Base. Within weeks after I found out about Carol's affair, between school, flying, and staff work, my plate was overflowing. Carol's boyfriend dumped her, and she didn't want to move forward with our divorce, even though I had a firm date next year for an assignment thousands of miles away at the Pentagon.

Life with Carol was a struggle, as we were still living in the same house and I didn't trust her to take care of the finances associated with our home. Because I was still married to Carol, the Air Force held me responsible for her well-being, per regulations. I also was in the middle of a term at the University of Southern California, working toward my master's degree at night and on weekends. I felt completely maxed out. I didn't need anything else to deal with.

"Bruce, this is Caroline." It was my sister on the phone. "You need to go see Mom. The cleaning lady called and found her drunk on the floor. She doesn't know what to do and Dad is on a business trip. He's traveling today and I'm too far away. You need to go see her now."

Caroline sounded frantic. She lived in the San Francisco Bay Area, hundreds of miles away from Mom and Dad. I abruptly excused myself from work and made the hours-long drive through afternoon Los Angeles traffic, all the time worrying about whether Mom was in serious trouble this time or whether she was "just drunk."

I got there as the sun was going down and walked up to my parents' townhouse. The front door was open — this didn't look good. I entered the house and turned the corner in the hallway. There was Dad. He had just arrived home from his trip to find Mom drunk and incoherent. I looked at Mom and was angry and disgusted. I was also relieved she wasn't seriously hurt or even worse. Dad gave me that tired, resigned look I'd seen so many times before. He told me he could deal with her from this point. I asked him if he needed any help. He said no, he was okay, and I should probably get back on the road for the drive home because traffic was bad.

I didn't even argue with him. I just didn't want to be around that entire situation. I told Dad I loved him, and I turned around and headed back out the door. This may have been the lowest point of my adult life. School, work, flying, and dealing with my divorce were nearly too much for me. And now there was this in-my-face reminder of my Mom's alcoholism. Instead of being a support when I could have used it, Mom was the same old burden as always with her drinking. I got in my car and drove away. I felt numb on the way home. About halfway there I started crying softly. It was the first time I had cried for many years. It was just overwhelming.

The next day, I called Dad to make sure Mom was okay. She was, he assured me. She was recovering from her drinking bout. My colleagues in the scheduling office asked me about my Mom. They were concerned because I left work so suddenly. I told them it was a false alarm and she's much better. I couldn't tell them what really happened. I didn't want to go anywhere near that.

Chapter 18

Reflections on My Divorce

Sunrise. Moving forward as a new day begins. (pexels.com)

As 1983 turned into 1984, my plate was full with school, flying, and scheduling. It was just too much to deal with all of that and try to make progress on getting a divorce from someone who didn't want to move on. Eventually, I grew tired of being in limbo, especially with a deadline rapidly approaching. In mid-1983, I had received a follow-on assignment to work at the Pentagon as an Air Staff Training (ASTRA) officer — a very prestigious position.

This made Carol regret her actions even more, as my departure date approached in the summer of 1984. I believe Carol would have been pleased if I departed March Air Force Base without our divorce being settled. That way, she could have her house in Southern California while I, as her husband, was still legally bound to support her from 3,000 miles away. She could have her cake and eat it, too.

I ramped up my efforts toward completing the divorce at the beginning of 1984. Carol continued to resist. When she realized she couldn't make me stop, she tried to get everything she could out of the settlement. That part, I could understand. She didn't see how she would make it without a husband to take care of her, even though she had a job that paid nearly as well as mine. We ended up parting on what I believe were reasonable terms for the both of us. I had loved her once and, on some level, I will always love her. The years we were dating and married in Upper Michigan were wonderful and I have fond memories of Carol. I will always keep that time in my heart.

I learned much from this episode in my life. I learned I am stronger and more resilient than I ever imagined. I received a devastating emotional blow from the woman I loved, and I recovered stronger than ever with my honor and reputation intact. I went through a painful divorce (is there any other kind?) and came out whole on the other side. I proved I could do damn near anything if I put my mind to it. I also faced one of a man's greatest fears — the unfaithfulness of his wife — and it did not incapacitate me. Instead, I overcame it. I survived.

I also realized the need to look at my part in this painful episode. Everything is a co-creation, especially in a relationship as intimate as a marriage. What caused the breakup? What was I doing wrong? Was I not doing something I should have? I've asked myself these questions. After some soul-searching and introspection, I've come to a few conclusions.

For one thing, I'm sure I didn't communicate as effectively or as much as I could have. I tend to "go inside" when interpersonal conflict arises — thinking about what is happening and making sense of it in my mind — rather than facing the source of the conflict and addressing issues right then. Carol was an avoider, too, so that just insured we weren't going to talk about painful stuff.

In my second marriage, consciously or subconsciously, I married "a talker." JoAnn will let me know the minute something is going awry, which is a good thing. I've also made progress in speaking my mind. I'm sure part of my improvement is because we've been married for 29+ years and our relationship has developed. I also know we've both worked on our communication. While I'll be the first to admit I still have a way to go, I feel we're in a good place.

Related to a lack of communication, though, I suspect Carol and I weren't on the same wavelength regarding our expectations. Part of the reason things came to a head at March was because I became more engaged in my Air Force career. In addition to my flying duties, I volunteered to become a squadron flight scheduler. That move would help my career by exposing me to another facet of squadron operations. I would get to know wing and squadron leadership in this role and they would get to know me. Being a scheduler was a full-time job by itself, with time set aside for maintaining my flying skills.

I also chose to pursue a master's degree at night. This required me to devote one or two evenings a week to class, along with twice that time doing homework and projects. I saw this as the perfect opportunity to get my master's — an unwritten requirement for promotion to lieutenant colonel in the Air Force — since it would take me just two years to complete it if I started right away. I also knew work and family demands would only increase as I became more senior in rank and we had children (which we both wanted).

Carol was 29 when we moved to Southern California. She had a college degree and a career of her own as a registered nurse. Carol still had something of a small-town perspective when I married her, though. She grew up on a farm in Illinois and worked in a very rural part of Michigan when we met. Even though I was in the Air Force while we dated, I'm not 100 percent certain she completely understood what the life of an Air Force officer entailed. KI Sawyer was a small, isolated Air Force base in the middle of the forest.

March, on the other hand, was a larger base, with a major headquarters in addition to the flying squadrons. A much bigger change was that we were now in a very urban, Southern California location just outside of Riverside. Carol had never lived in "the big city" before. Even though we had more than a few discussions about it before moving to March, she may also not have realized the increasing time demands on me as I pursued an Air Force career. In hindsight, I expect our move must have been disorienting for her.

I must also share responsibility for the limited time we spent together after we moved to Southern California. Between my full-time day job, occasionally flying at night, going to class one or two nights a week, and Carol's shift work at the hospital, we spent less time with each other than we had when I was simply a line pilot at KI Sawyer, even though I lived one week out of three away from home on alert. The lack of opportunity to reinforce the bonds between us likely contributed to our drifting apart.

Carol was also turning 30 not long after our arrival at March and I remember she was upset by this — she worried about getting older. She considered herself overweight, too. She weighed more than she wanted ever since I met her. Her weight never made any difference to me. I never, ever said anything to her about it, though, but I know it bothered her a lot.

I expect the combination of her getting older and perhaps feeling unattractive because of her weight made her more vulnerable to another man flirting with her as John did at the VA Hospital where she worked. This is no excuse for her behavior, but it might help explain why she would have even considered doing what she did. The bottom line for me, though, was there was no way I could stay with Carol. I didn't trust her any more.

My experience with divorce also helped solidify what I was looking for in a wife. I knew I wanted someone I could trust. I knew I wanted a partner who would communicate easily with me. I knew I wanted a wife who understood what it might take for me to succeed as an Air Force officer and would support me on that journey. JoAnn was all these things and much, much more — as you will read later in this book. I appreciate that my experience with Carol helped me clarify what I wanted in my second marriage. I hope she also grew from our experience.

Chapter 19

General Officer Investigation

My official photo taken before assuming command of the 19th Air Refueling Group at Robins Air Force Base, Georgia in 1999. I was a brand-new colonel. (U.S. Air Force)

"I'm sending Brigadier General Starbuck to your group tomorrow. He'll be doing a full investigation of your personnel processes to see what caused this problem. I expect you to provide him with everything he needs."

I received the news from my three-star commanding officer. It was 1999, and I had been in command of the 19th Air Refueling Group for four months. Lieutenant General Hopper was sending his deputy, a brigadier general, to perform a full-scale investigation into my group's performance reporting and promotion recommendation system. He was doing this because one of the majors in my group filed a formal written complaint.

There was no way I could put a happy face on this — the best my group and I could do was "break even." The worst that could happen was the officers in charge, including me, could be unceremoniously relieved of command. And the worst part of all this was that I knew the major's complaint was legitimate.

My divorce emphasized how important truthfulness and integrity are in my personal and professional life. After that experience, I recommitted to always being straight forward with my colleagues and my family. This can be hard to do sometimes, especially when confronted with a disagreeable policy or a difficult situation.

In the Air Force, there's a saying that "you live and die by your reputation." If you have a reputation as an honest, straight-forward leader, people will give you the benefit of the doubt. They will allow you a great deal of leeway and trust you're doing what's right. You're seen as believable because you've earned it.

On the other side of the coin, if an officer is caught lying, his or her reputation is shot. If they aren't fired outright, their word is suspect. Everything they say is checked out. Their every move is verified and double-checked. It's a terrible place to be and, thankfully, I learned early on I never wanted to go there.

Growing up in my family, despite not dealing with my mother's drinking, we were truthful with each other. There was never any doubt we could trust each other, no matter what. That still is true today between my brothers, my sister, and me.

When I realized Carol was lying in the worst way possible, I understood the impact of a loss of integrity and what that does to a person's reputation. How does a person recover from a severe lack of integrity?

Unfortunately, integrity and trust issues plagued some of my colleagues during my career, both in the Air Force and afterward. As 19th Air Refueling Group (ARG) commander, I had to correct lingering integrity issues left over from my predecessor. Without quick, corrective action from me, they could have had a lasting, negative impact on the group, and taken me down, too.

One particular issue came to my attention within the first month of my command as I received orientation into my new position. It had to do with officer promotion, performance reporting, and officer assignment integrity — three sensitive issues for the Air Force and all the other military services as well. Unlike in the corporate world, all Air Force officer positions are filled from within — a colonel or general cannot be hired from the "outside" to fill critical, national security leadership roles. The complete integrity of the promotion system is essential. Even a perception of favoritism or impropriety threatens the system's validity, and the Air Force deals with violations quickly and severely.

The Air Force promotion system works by creating a promotion recommendation form (PRF) for each officer when their records meet a selection board for promotion to the next rank. While there are early and late promotions for those who have excelled or officers whom the board believes have earned a promotion despite being passed over earlier, the Air Force selects the vast majority of officers for promotion when their year group is "in-the-primary-zone" (IPZ). An officer only competes once for IPZ promotion to each rank, so it's a very big deal.

The PRF is the single most important document that meets the board. The one-sheet PRF, written by an officer's commander, designates whether he or she gets a "definitely promote" (DP) or "promote" (P) recommendation. DP recommendations are very small in number and limited by quota — an officer getting a DP when competing in-the-primary-zone will get promoted. The Air Force instituted the DP/P system in the late 1980s to ensure commanding officers had a viable way to identify their top performers when those officers meet promotion boards.

Almost all officers who do not get a DP get a promote recommendation. Officers who receive a promote recommendation have to rely on their accumulated annual officer performance reports (OPRs) and duty history and hope their records are strong enough for them to advance. Duty history assessment from promotion-board members, primarily focused on the current position an officer holds, can make-or-break an officer's promotion chances.

Within any organization, there are certain leadership positions viewed as being "promotable." By placing an officer in one of these key positions, the commander is sending a message he/she has trust in the leadership and abilities of that officer to perform well in their assigned role. The competition for DPs and assignment to key positions is stiff, as you might imagine. I created an appendix (Appendix B) to this book that provides a more detailed description of Air Force ranks and additional promotion specifics if you're interested in finding out more. This can all feel like it's a bit much to understand — it took me years to figure this stuff out.

Within a week after I took command of the 19th Air Refueling Group, I saw I had two majors assigned to the same position as Chief of Standardization and Evaluation Division — one of the key leadership roles on my group staff. Not only that, both officers had performance reports written by my predecessor describing their achievements and responsibilities in that specific job for the same time period.

If my predecessor did this knowingly, this was a clear integrity breach — two officers cannot be chief of a division for the same reporting period. The most charitable interpretation was this was a situation where the previous commander was asleep at the wheel and wasn't aware of what he was doing. The less charitable interpretation was this could have been a deliberate attempt on his part to mislead the upcoming promotion board in favor of the major who was not performing those duties. Regardless of the cause, this situation reflected unfavorably on the previous commander.

As soon as I found out about this contradiction, I reassigned one of the two majors to another position within the group. I also wrestled with what I should do to correct the record. I chose to fix the current situation and leave it at that since the previous actions had occurred before my taking command.

Fast forward to four months later. I'm making decisions regarding which of my majors meeting the lieutenant colonel promotion board I will submit for a definitely promote recommendation, with the remainder getting promote recommendations. Because the number of 19 ARG majors up for promotion on this board was small, my boss (an Air Force three-star general) "aggregated" my IPZ majors into a larger pool of officers under his command so he could give a reasonable number of DPs to the entire number. Still, as any good commander would, he asked his subordinate (me) for recommendations regarding who should get the expected one DP from my unit. I gave him my recommendation, along with justification for why I felt that way. The general took my recommendation and awarded the DP to the major I recommended — the only one my officers got.

Right after my IPZ majors received notification of their promotion recommendations, one of them met me at the bottom of the air stairs when I returned from a three-day trip to Randolph Air Force Base in Texas. The officer wanted to have a private discussion in my office. It was a Saturday afternoon, and the major looked very serious, so I told him to follow me to the headquarters building and we would talk right then.

Once we arrived, he showed me his PRF — he had received a promote (not a DP) recommendation. He then handed me the letter he intended to send to the 21st Air Force commander, my boss. The major wanted a full Inspector General (IG) investigation into the officer performance reports of two other majors from the 19 ARG who were meeting the promotion board. These were the same two officers who had OPRs for the Chief of Standardization and Evaluation position over the same time period — the situation I described earlier. One of those two officers had received the lone DP given to my group.

The major's question was what to do next. It concerned him that having an IG investigation descend upon the group would be highly disruptive and cause us to look bad (yes and yes — his concerns were justified, and I knew it). Should he send the letter, he asked?

I knew this would be a mess. A full-blown IG investigation could have a disastrous effect on how my boss and those above him viewed my performance, especially since I was still new in the job. Far more important than any effect on me, what were the negative repercussions this might have on the people in my group?

At that moment, I would have been ecstatic to see this whole issue just go away, regardless of what I thought of my predecessor. There was just no way this could be a "win" for my group — the best we could hope for was to break even. Despite my concerns, I knew in my heart there was only one right answer. And it wasn't difficult to come to that decision. My integrity, the integrity of my group, and the integrity of the Air Force promotion system were being challenged.

I told the major he was within his rights to question the situation and the most appropriate person to send the letter to was the 21st Air Force commander, Lieutenant General Hopper. The major also asked me for advice on the wording of the letter. I recommended he take out some emotion and stick to the facts as he knew them and just leave it at that — let the general decide to investigate or not (although I knew the answer to that without even asking).

The major indicated he would revise the letter and mail it the next day. I asked him if it would be okay to provide me with a copy, so I could give the general a heads-up this was coming his way. That way, my boss could prepare for its arrival and act quickly, as this whole issue was time-sensitive, with the promotion board meeting soon. The major agreed and the next day he handed me a copy just before he mailed his signed letter. I called my boss and faxed him the letter.

As expected, General Hopper's reaction was swift and direct. The general would send his deputy, Brigadier General Starbuck, to spend three days at my group taking sworn testimony from all parties involved. He would also conduct a thorough review of the procedures we use for writing and processing officer evaluations in the group. The next morning, I called in my commanders and administrative staff to tell them what was going on. The general's investigation surprised and scared them. They worried they might be found guilty of violating some procedure in their haste to process the myriad of performance reports and other materials they're required to handle daily. Who knows what the investigation might turn up? The "going in perception" was that the 19 ARG looked as if we had violated regulations.

I assured them our responsibility was to tell the complete truth. Be forthright. Don't hide anything. If there were mistakes, it's far better to volunteer that information, rather than hope the general doesn't find them. I then made a point of assigning my deputy as the general's escort officer. He was not to interfere with the general's investigation, nor attempt to "sit in" on any of the depositions. His role was to insure the general had access to everyone and everything he needed to conduct his investigation. Period.

General Starbuck arrived on Tuesday, the day after General Hopper ordered the investigation. He spent the next three days interviewing everyone who touched performance reports, from the young airmen in the admin shop to me as the group commander. The general was thorough and, I must admit, a bit unnerving when he asked me to provide sworn, taped testimony to a series of investigation questions. After the three days, General Starbuck flew home to McGuire Air Force Base. Before he left, he told us once he filed his report, the 21st Air Force commander would advise us of any actions he would take resulting from the investigation. After he departed, we waited for the other shoe to drop. Not fun, but not unbearable, either.

Once General Starbuck turned in his report, there were no negative repercussions for the group resulting from the investigation, for which we were all grateful. General Hopper didn't fire anyone or remove people from positions of responsibility. He didn't insert negative statements in our performance reports, either. I also believe there was a positive result to this episode — General Starbuck, the investigating officer, came away with a good impression of the group. My interactions with him after that point were all upbeat.

As part of the follow-up to the investigation, they asked me to review the recommendation for the one major in my group who had the DP. I convinced General Hopper the major was still deserving of the DP regardless of mistakes made on his previous performance report. The major got to keep his DP and his performance report remained the same.

The major that raised the issue did not end up getting get a DP. As much as I liked him, his record just didn't justify it. The third major, the one who was the "other" major assigned to the Chief of Standardization and Evaluation position, had a new performance report issued reflecting the lesser role he had been performing in. He also got a "promote" recommendation. Despite being recognized as deserving officers with substantial potential, because of the competitive nature of lieutenant colonel promotions, the two majors who received "promote" recommendations were passed over for promotion and retired earlier than they would have liked. The major with the DP became a lieutenant colonel.

Outside the 19 ARG, the results were less encouraging. While I didn't see the investigation report, I'm sure it didn't reflect well on my predecessor's performance. He had an impressive career and appeared on the brigadier general promotion list two years after this incident. Unfortunately for him, I understand the senator from Georgia who sat on the Senate Armed Services Committee (SASC) refused to approve his promotion, citing lack of integrity. The SASC is the congressional committee that approves military promotions. The senator had been the congressional representative from the district that included Robins AFB and the 19 ARG in 1999. As a congressman, he remembered the general officer investigation of the 19 ARG and knew the results. The senator held up the entire promotion list until the Air Force removed my predecessor's name. During my Air Force career that's the only time I recall ever seeing a promotion list held up solely to remove one name.

This incident highlights the importance of integrity. I'm grateful I approached this situation from a clear-headed and heartfelt perspective. While I doubt I ever thought of Carol during this entire episode, the negative experience I had with her reinforced the critical importance of keeping integrity paramount. I chose to remedy a complicated "two officers in the same position" situation because it was the right thing to do. I didn't attempt to talk the major out of sending a complaint to my boss even though I knew my group and I would be subjected to an extensive investigation. And I gave my group instructions to provide the complete truth even if it took the investigating general into areas unrelated to the original investigation. If I had approached this situation any other way, I would rightfully have been skewered, although I had nothing to do with the original violation.

Chapter 20

Top Secret

*KC-135 tanker and B-52 bomber conducting air refueling training
for the Single Integrated Operational Plan strike mission.
(U.S. Air Force)*

"Sir, we have a big problem."

These are words no commander ever wants to hear.

My lead intelligence officer in the 19th Air Refueling Group, a young captain, stood in front of me in my office. It was mid-afternoon in the fall of 2000. She had arrived, unannounced and unscheduled, and it was clear she was upset.

"We're missing a Top Secret SIOP planning document. I went to retrieve it from the safe in the Plans Division and it wasn't there. It wasn't checked out to anyone in the shop and we couldn't find it.

"We need to inform Strategic Command that it has been compromised."

The Single Integrated Operational Plan (SIOP) document was what bomber/tanker aircrews, missile officers, and nuclear missile submarine crews used to execute a retaliatory strike in response to a nuclear attack against the United States. If it was in the hands of an enemy who intended to launch a surprise attack against us, our intercontinental ballistic missiles

(ICBMs), sea-launched ballistic missiles (SLBMs) and nuclear bombers might be in danger.

By immediately raising the issue that "our SIOP plans have been compromised" to United States Strategic Command, we would be sounding a red alarm. They would likely have had no choice but to provide an emergency reissue of planning documents to our nuclear forces throughout the world. Because of the nature of the threat, I expect our nuclear forces might have even been placed in a higher state of readiness.

A change like that would immediately have been noticed by our allies and adversaries alike. Depending on a huge number of internal and external factors working on each of the countries involved, their responses could range from relative indifference to increasing their own state of readiness in response to what we just did. While all of this was speculation, it was not hard to imagine a plausible scenario where things quickly ratcheted up to dangerous levels.

Obviously, I did not want to send a "compromised plans" message to Strategic Command. By far the most important reason was that I did not want to create extraordinary turmoil to our nuclear forces, with second- and third-order effects having potential international repercussions.

This incident would reflect badly on my command, but that was of secondary importance. While I was not personally involved, nor had I given any guidance that would have allowed this to happen, the fact was, I was the commander. Everyone who takes command of a military unit understands they are responsible for the success or failure of the organization. This failure would have fallen directly on me, which is exactly how it should be.

Yet, I could not dismiss the possibility of espionage out-of-hand, even though the chances of that were extremely remote. I knew that not many years before, a naval officer named Walker had been arrested for selling classified technology and operational deployment information to the Soviet Union. The volume and nature of the information he provided allowed the Soviets to make great leaps forward in their weapons development. He also gave them enough information about the location and nature of our forces that the United States would have been at a serious disadvantage at the outset of a conflict.

Walker's motivation was financial. He was not an ideologue, nor did he display a bad attitude. Until his arrest, nobody suspected a thing. While I couldn't identify anyone in my group who might be a threat, the consequences of a compromise were severe, and I needed to take it seriously.

Another consideration was the situation in the world at that time. In 2000, Russia was still reeling from the collapse of the Soviet Union, and China didn't have a large or potent enough nuclear arsenal to seriously threaten us without being assured of total obliteration. Our relations with both countries were adversarial, but not combative. It made no sense that either of them would risk a preemptive strike against us. North Korea had no nuclear weapons, so that wasn't a consideration. The other nuclear powers in the world were either allies or unaligned nations.

The captain's motivations seemed clear. She was a good officer, very competent in performing her job. She discovered what appeared to be a serious security breach and she was performing her duty as best she could. She had informed me, and her recommendation was clear and direct — send this information up the chain of command immediately.

While she didn't state this, it was apparent she didn't want to be held responsible for any delay associated with supplying this information to higher headquarters. The underlying message to me was that I needed to approve her recommendation, or she would inform headquarters through her intelligence channels. She would be within her rights to do that, too.

I took all of this into account as I composed my response for the captain. I asked her what she had done to find the document prior to coming to me. Once she gave me a rundown, I proposed the following:

"This obviously is a very serious situation and I appreciate you bringing it to my attention immediately. I can't help but think the document is there in the Plans Division and we just haven't found it yet. Give me twenty-four hours. If we haven't found it by then, I will inform Strategic Command. I take full responsibility."

That last line convinced her to back off from the urgency to inform higher command immediately. She would not be held liable for any delays in telling headquarters. I would be the one responsible if and when any punishment came down.

I told her I would see her tomorrow at the same time. She left and I picked up the phone. I called my Chief of Plans, a highly experienced lieutenant colonel who ran our Plans Division. Capable and responsive, I knew he would do whatever was necessary. His rear end was on the line, too.

"Bob, I need you to see me now. Bring one of your officers with you. I need your best. Someone who is experienced. Whatever they're doing, this becomes their Number One priority right now. Do you understand?"

"Yes, sir. We'll be right there."

Ten minutes later, Lieutenant Colonel Bob Hurt walked into my office with Major Chuck Mullis. Bob was the Chief of the 19 ARG Plans Division, and Chuck was one of his most capable officers. Both officers were career navigators. They were also seasoned, experienced, and highly professional. Bob had made an excellent choice in Chuck. He was the right guy for what I had in mind. After I told them to close the door behind them, I spoke to Lt Col Hurt.

"I am directing Major Mullis to perform a full investigation into the missing document. That is his primary job from this moment forward. No later than twenty-four hours from now, I want him to report back to me with what he found. You (Lt Col Hurt) are to provide him with everything he needs. You will also make all your people available to Major Mullis as he requests. No exceptions. Do you have any questions?"

"No, sir. I understand."

I then asked Lt Col Hurt to leave, which he did promptly. I needed to give Major Mullis specific instructions. Because Lt Col Hurt might conceivably be at fault, I wanted to be sure Major Mullis had a good understanding of what I wanted him to do. I spoke again.

"Chuck, I need you to find that document. Tear the room apart if you need to — we can put things back together afterwards. You have twenty-four hours to do this. You know all hell will break loose if we can't locate it."

"Yes, sir."

"You report directly to me on this. Not my deputy, not Bob Hurt. I don't want you telling anyone else about your findings. Just me. We have to do this completely by the book. Don't cut corners. If we can't find it by tomorrow this time, we have to assume that someone, intentionally or unintentionally, took it out of the secure area. If that's the case, I will immediately report it to Strategic Command and my boss at 21st Air Force. Do you understand?"

"Yes, sir."

"Your primary job is to find the document. You also need to trace back who last touched it and when. We need to establish a timeline for the chain of control. Don't speculate. Gather facts. If we've actually lost it, we'll all need to testify and you and I both have to be armed with the truth, not conjecture. Any questions?"

"No, sir."

"Thanks, Chuck. Good luck."

Major Mullis saluted, turned around, and left the room. I knew I had an excellent officer investigating this. He was extremely knowledgeable about the Plans Division — he was aware of all the processes and the physical aspects of the secure area. I also realized I had put him in a very difficult position. I was asking him to investigate his friends and colleagues.

Furthermore, I had placed him directly in the line of fire. If push came to shove and guilty parties needed to be identified, he would have had to do everything completely correct — no mistakes. His actions, his conclusions, his line of reasoning, and his personal motives (and perhaps even his culpability as a key officer within the Plans Division) would be reviewed in detail and maybe even questioned in a military court.

I had to rely on him completely. A great deal depended on it. The military relies heavily on its people safeguarding classified materials. Top Secret is the highest classification level, and failure to keep track of those materials can easily result in ended careers, early retirement or discharge, and in extreme cases, even fines or imprisonment. While I felt I had decided upon a responsible course of action and that I had good officers and NCOs working hard to find the document, I prayed my faith in the professionalism and reliability of my people would be rewarded.

The next day dragged on. I had plenty to keep me occupied, but I couldn't help thinking about how the investigation was going. I purposely chose not to contact Major Mullis — I didn't want to be perceived as applying undue command influence. I had given him his orders and I'm sure he was carrying them out as best he could. As the morning turned into afternoon, I began to allow myself a little anxiety. No news was definitely not good news in this case.

Then, at 1:00, I saw Major Mullis at my office doorway. He smiled.

"Sir, we found the planning document."

"Thank God," I said as I exhaled. "Where was it?"

It turned out that our Top Secret safe, while a reliably secure piece of equipment, had a significant flaw. Evidently, when closing one of the upper drawers, a document that's not fully secured in a folder could fall down in the gap between the drawers and the back of the safe. If the positioning of the drawers was just right, the document could end up in the bottom of the safe underneath the very bottom drawer. The guys in the Plans Division had to semi-dismantle the safe to check that area. When they did, they discovered the document. With decades of experience in classified plans, no one could ever remember this type of thing happening before.

It was clear to me that given the location of the document and the group nature of the discovery process, the document had been secure the entire time it was unaccounted for. Nothing had been compromised.

I called the captain from intelligence and asked her to come to my office. I wanted to follow up with her, since she was a key part of this incident. After she arrived, I asked Major Mullis to describe to her what he discovered. She was relieved, too. She didn't want to be the bearer of bad news any more than the rest of us. I thanked Major Mullis and the captain for doing an excellent job. I then asked Major Mullis to write up his findings in a report. I intended to provide this information to my boss. Other Air Force organizations that used this same type of safe would need to know about this incident. Later that day, I called my commander and told him about what had occurred over the last 24 hours. I also told him a report would be forthcoming.

Unfortunately, this wasn't the end of this incident. A couple weeks after we found the document and the case was put to bed, I received a call from a reporter for *The Macon Telegraph* (our local newspaper). He asked me about the missing Top Secret document. The reporter had detailed information and knew about the investigation process we went through. It was obvious someone from my Plans Division had communicated with him.

I patiently described what we had done, without confirming our processes, procedures, and capabilities. I was completely honest, but only spoke in generalities, as the rest of what he asked about was the nature of our operations, our flying mission, and the extent of our capabilities. This fell in the category of Essential Elements of Friendly Information (EEFI) and it was incumbent upon me to safeguard that as commander.

It bothered me that one of my people would feel compelled to talk with a newspaper reporter about our internal processes, especially since our investigation found the document was secured the entire time and nobody had acted neglectfully. It was clearly an equipment malfunction.

I called our base public relations section and informed them of what just happened. I also described my response and they confirmed I handled the situation appropriately. I then called Bob Hurt and told him about what occurred. I also asked him if he had any idea who might be behind this. He was taken aback. No one came immediately to mind. I ended the call by telling him that perhaps this was just a one-off and the reporter would be satisfied with what I just told him. No such luck.

The next day, I received another call from the same reporter. He had questions related specifically to the responses I provided the day before. His detailed questions clearly came from someone with an intimate knowledge of what happened. A member of the Plans Division or someone who was familiar with what happened had to be in active conversation with the reporter, feeding him questions to ask me. Once again, I provided him with truthful but generalized responses. I would not provide him with EEFI, and I would not agree to his conclusion that my group had committed a grave error and put the entire country at risk due to our careless neglect. I had the distinct feeling this reporter felt he was on the verge of breaking a Watergate-level scandal.

After I hung up, I decided I needed to address this issue directly with the Plans Division. I called Lieutenant Colonel Hurt, told him what just transpired, and asked him to assemble his entire team in the secure area so I could talk with them. I also wanted any other group members who had accessed that document over the past 60 days to be present. He agreed. This was a relatively small group, 10 people at the most. We set the meeting for the next morning at 0900. I knew I needed to choose my words carefully, because I was acutely aware someone in the room would tell the reporter everything I said.

As I entered the secure area, the room came to attention. I asked them to be at ease and take a seat around the large conference table in the adjoining room. I wanted this to be more of an informal discussion than anything else. I thought if the team understood what occurred, they would know no one intentionally violated any policies or disregarded any procedures. I also wanted to confirm to them why I believed the document was safe and secure the entire time, even though no one was able to lay their hands on it for a short period.

I described my conversations with the newspaper reporter from Macon, and sensed the room tensing up. I emphasized I was not interested in who had been talking with him. In fact, everyone in the room had the right, as American citizens, to talk about whatever they wanted, within the bounds set by Air Force authorities. I explained that by giving information on policies, procedures, operational priorities, and the nature of our mission, even if the individual pieces were unclassified, they were potentially providing enough information that our mission success and safety could be jeopardized. As their commander, our safety and success were my highest priorities. I was concerned the individual who was calling the reporter was risking that.

I then answered a few questions regarding the incident. I closed by asking them to talk with Lieutenant Colonel Hurt or come see me if they thought of something else later or if they had any concerns they didn't want to raise in front of everyone else. The mood of the meeting had changed from where it began. I believed they now understood I wasn't hiding anything. More importantly, they saw I was on their side and I wanted them to succeed.

From that point forward, the calls from the reporter stopped. No news stories ever appeared, and I never heard anything further about the incident. This incident reinforced several lessons for me. It showed me the importance of taking a step back, looking at a situation in its entirety, and resisting the urge to act upon a worst-case scenario. For example, if I had agreed to the captain's conclusion that we needed to send an emergency report to Strategic Command immediately, the consequences could have been disastrous, and we would have looked like idiots when the document was eventually found.

It also showed me how important it was to trust my people. I had to believe in my division chief Bob Hurt, and place my complete confidence in my investigating officer Chuck Mullis. Without their dedicated, calm, professional behavior, the situation could have easily gone off the rails.

Finally, this incident showed me the importance of treating people like adults. Explaining the situation to them as best I knew it. Taking them into my confidence by talking to them in a reasoned manner. Treating them with the respect due them as accomplished professionals.

This incident also reinforced how blessed I was to have such wonderful men and women under my command. We could never have made it through this without each other.

Chapter 21

Standing Up

19th Air Refueling Group photo in 2000. I am second from the left in the front row. My Senior Enlisted Advisor, Chief Master Sergeant Garry Frost, is on my right and my deputy commander, Lieutenant Colonel Tom Stark, is on my left. Our group Black Knight statue is between me and Lt Col Stark. Members of my four squadrons, two KC-135s, and a C-141 are in the background. (U.S. Air Force)

"They're always watching you when you're their commander. They listen to everything you say. They see everything you do. They'll do anything for you, but you have to earn their loyalty and respect every single day."

Lieutenant Colonel Dayre Lias, Commander,
32nd Air Refueling Squadron (ARS)

From 1986-1988, I had the privilege of serving under one of the best leaders I've ever met, Lt Col Dayre Lias, the commander of the 32 ARS at

Barksdale AFB in Louisiana. I was a KC-10 instructor pilot and one of four flight commanders in his squadron. It was during this time, with his support, that the Air Force selected me for early promotion to major.

Lt Col Lias was highly regarded by all of us for his outstanding flying skills — he was my primary instructor when I first qualified in the KC-10 in 1982 -- yet his greatest assets were his integrity and focused leadership. He was approachable, but knew he needed to keep an appropriate distance. He was conscious of his position, but not aloof.

I have a number of great stories about Lt Col Lias, including the time when he and I were both on a panel of mid-level officers convened to provide feedback to Strategic Air Command leadership on how best to improve the command — I was one of a handful of younger officers and he was the panel lead as the senior officer/squadron commander. The number one recommendation from our panel was to eliminate air divisions from SAC — I believe I was even the one who initially suggested this change. There were no dissenting opinions during our discussions. It was unanimous. We felt air divisions were an unnecessary relic of the 1950s Curtis LeMay Era and provided a useless level of leadership between the aircrews and SAC leadership.

The problem was that the chairman of this entire review was a brigadier general air division commander. Our primary recommendation pointed to the conclusion that the general was in a useless job. As our panel lead, Lt Col Lias had to make a presentation describing our panel's recommendations to the general and other senior officers. We could tell he, understandably, wasn't 100 percent comfortable briefing our conclusion that the general's job needed to go away. He also knew we were watching him to see what he did as our leader.

The time came, and he gave an excellent briefing. He listed our recommendations in priority order, along with our reasoning behind each one. He was respectful, but he didn't try to shade our findings to make them more palatable. The general, to his credit, didn't take things personally and promised to present our recommendations to the commander of SAC in their entirety. A few months later, SAC announced it was eliminating all of its air divisions. I credit SAC leadership with acting upon this and many of our other recommendations, too . . .

"I think that this situation absolutely requires a really futile and stupid gesture be done on somebody's part."

Otter Stratton, a fictional character from the movie
"Animal House"

"And we're just the guys to do it."

Bluto Blutarsky, a (hopefully) fictional character
from the same movie.

The movie *Animal House* came out in 1978, the year I went on active duty in the Air Force, and since then I have used this quote from the movie extensively.

In fact, I witnessed "a really futile gesture" in real life once. I saw my squadron commander stand up in front of a theater full of people and point out hypocritical behavior from the Strategic Air Command Inspector General (IG) during a disastrous Operational Readiness Inspection (ORI) debriefing. The audience included wing leadership and a large team of SAC inspectors, including numerous colonels and general officers.

My squadron commander performed this "futile gesture," knowing there was zero chance his remarks would be seen as anything other than sharp criticism. This possibly contributed to an early end to his career — he retired shortly thereafter. Yet those of us in his squadron admired how he stood up for what he believed was right. I've remembered this ever since, and I hope I have lived up to his example throughout my life.

In the spring of 1980, I was a lieutenant copilot and we in the 410th Bomb Wing at KI Sawyer AFB in Upper Michigan had an Operational Readiness Inspection (ORI). Each unit in SAC was required to have an ORI every two years. SAC ORIs were extremely stressful for an organization — everything from aircraft generation to flying performance to unit administration was evaluated. A huge team of inspectors would land on a base and the inspection would last a couple of weeks, culminating in a mass exercise, whereby all available aircraft would launch in a minimum interval takeoff and fly missions simulating the Single Integrated Operational Plan. While an outstanding grade could make a career, a failing grade would certainly end it. We all knew that.

The ORI started off well. Then, disaster hit. Literally. During a bomb load of a B-52, a munitions loading crew accidentally dropped one of the simulated bombs. The bomb was damaged. If this had happened to a genuine weapon, it would have been rendered ineffective and potentially could have leaked radiation.

When we heard about this accident through the rumor mill, we all knew what it meant. We had failed. It wouldn't matter if we did everything else perfectly. Because our team had damaged a (simulated) weapon, we could not pass the mission phase of the evaluation, which meant failure overall.

We still completed all phases of the ORI, and the flying portion went well — all KC-135 air refuelings were successful and all B-52 bomb runs were right on target. Yet, the tone of the evaluation changed dramatically after the bomb accident. The evaluators focused on finding things to justify failing us, rather than looking for ways we could improve. Once the two-week inspection was complete, we all gathered in the base theater to hear the results. We knew it was going to be bad. This became even more apparent when we saw the array of SAC generals in the front row of the theater, waiting to hear the results. If we had passed, they wouldn't have flown in for the debrief.

It went as expected. Lots of critical remarks, most of which were focused on the dropped simulated bomb. We also received criticism for many things that would never have been mentioned otherwise. The IG team went out of their way to paint a picture of a unit that was failing. Even though no one in the audience spoke up, I could tell many of my squadron colleagues and friends were resentful. They thought it was grossly unfair to paint all of us as failures.

It was when the SAC colonel on stage began to question our integrity that things got ugly. He cited an incident in which a senior pilot (from another base in SAC) had been disciplined because he carried a small sail boat back to home station on an otherwise empty KC-135 redeploying to base. By even bringing that up, he implied that we in the KC-135 community were lacking in integrity. There was a palpable sense of anger in the audience.

This is when my squadron commander stood up and began to speak. He was not called upon. He just did it. He told the colonel that his remarks were unfair and unwarranted. He said he was proud to be a KC-135 squadron commander and he was proud of his squadron. Furthermore, he was familiar with that incident and knew the officer in question. While the pilot may have used poor judgment, there was nothing prohibiting what he did. The regulation the colonel cited went into effect after the incident.

The SAC colonel attempted to justify his remarks, and he and my commander went back and forth for a few minutes. I could see the wing leadership was unhappy with my commander. They were already getting beaten up. They didn't need to have a disrespectful lieutenant colonel on top of everything else. Things started to come to a head.

Then, abruptly, my commander sat down. He had made his point. I think he also became concerned that some of us in the squadron would rise to his defense if he kept going. I'm sure he didn't want any of us to suffer collateral damage because of his actions.

I can't say whether my boss was passed over for promotion to colonel because of this, a deficiency in his record, or any other incidents in his past that may have had an effect. I do recall hearing he had been given a medal for heroism during the Vietnam War when, without permission, he risked his aircraft and his crew over North Vietnam to refuel a heavily damaged Navy fighter trying to get enough fuel for the pilot to bail out over the Gulf of Tonkin, where a Navy ship could rescue him. Because of my commander's actions, the fighter pilot was able to make it to safety and avoid capture. The Air Force didn't know whether to punish my boss or give him a medal. They decided on the latter; although, there may have been some lingering repercussions.

We were all watching him at the debrief in the base theater. I can tell you he was one of the most admired commanders I ever had — for many reasons, not just for standing up for what he believed was right that day. I've thought about his example many times during my career. I aspired to be a commander who would stand up against unfair treatment of his people, even if that decision was unpopular with senior leadership. And I would get my chance . . .

Near the end of my tour as 19th Air Refueling Group commander, an incident occurred with one of my crews while they were deployed in the Pacific. They redeployed through Hawaii. Air Mobility Command wanted them to go through Alaska. When they arrived in Hawaii, they were met by the Security Police, who escorted them to the base detention facility and interrogated them for hours. The SPs accused my crew of trying to hijack the plane for their own personal uses and threatened them with incarceration. I found this out, in the middle of the night, shortly after it happened. By the time I became aware, the crew had been released and were awaiting transport back home. We sent a replacement crew to Hawaii to fly their aircraft back to Robins AFB in Georgia.

In the meantime, Air Mobility Command (AMC) was pressuring me hard to take action against my captain aircraft commander and my major navigator. At the time, the KC-135s were still relatively new to AMC and the command hadn't fully integrated the tanker community into the global cargo network. My guys were returning from doing a trans-Pacific refueling mission and may not have even realized they were supposed to go to Alaska to pick up some cargo before returning home. I knew these officers well. They both were young, promising, highly professional fliers. It was inconceivable they would disobey instructions on a lark. There had to have been a misinterpretation or confusion or something else that caused this.

I tracked my two officers down in Hawaii and heard their side of what happened. What they told me was plausible. There was confusion regarding their role in the system. They didn't realize they failed to follow established procedures. They had flown the Pacific routes on refueling missions before and had never had to check in with the mobility cargo authority previously. They just planned on coming home since there were no more refueling missions to accomplish. That's what they were doing.

It wasn't long before I started receiving calls from general officers at AMC, including the 21st Air Force command section. While they couldn't tell me to punish my crew (if they directed punishment, that would have been exercising undue command influence on me), they hinted strongly I should make an example of my two officers. They wanted to send a message to all aircrews throughout AMC.

What they really wanted me to do was scapegoat my officers. I refused. I went toe-to-toe with three different generals that day. I told them the fault was with the AMC system. I said that after five years tankers hadn't yet been fully integrated into the system, our training was lacking, and something like this was bound to happen sooner or later. I knew that anything I did to punish these officers, even if it was informal, would end their careers. I told the generals the only way I would take any action against my officers would be if a formal investigation was conducted and my crewmembers were found negligent. Otherwise, we would correct the problem within the group by conducting local training of these crewmembers, and all other crewmembers under my command, to ensure everyone knew the proper procedures used to fly in the AMC cargo system.

My reaction tied their hands. They couldn't tell me what to do as the commander of these officers. The generals convened a formal investigation. An officer flew to Robins about a week later and interviewed me, my crews, our flight instructors, and other key people regarding our training process and how we prepared our crews to fly overseas. The investigating officer then travelled to Hawaii and Okinawa (where the flight originated) to interview people there.

After the investigation was completed, I repeatedly asked to see the results. While I was not entitled to see them, I hoped I would be able to look at the conclusions the investigating officer drew. I never received permission, partly because I departed a couple of months after this incident to go to Germany for a new assignment at U.S. European Command headquarters.

Most importantly, I did not receive any negative feedback regarding my two officers. I'm happy to report the two of them have had very successful careers in the Air Force. If I had bowed to the pressure to make an example of them, I would have cut short two promising careers and ruined two lives.

I don't know if any of this affected my career, but that's not even a consideration. If I had thrown my guys under the bus to save myself, I would never have been able to look at myself in the mirror. I would have seen myself as a coward. My entire group was watching me to see how I reacted to this situation; it was not just the two officers who were directly involved. I hope I demonstrated to all of them, just like my commanders did for me years before, how to stand up for the men and women under my command.

Chapter 22

Leadership Failure

(alacartespirit.com)

"What you're showing me is not what I want at all. I'm really disappointed in you."

It was 1988 and the Strategic Air Command (SAC) Director of Personnel, an Air Force colonel, stopped me in the middle of my presentation. My boss asked him what was wrong. This was our fourth attempt in two weeks to present a command briefing to the colonel. We only had a week left before we would give our presentation to the four-star Commander-in-Chief of Strategic Air Command and the SAC headquarters directorate chiefs — all the generals at SAC HQ. The colonel, my boss's boss, had rejected all previous attempts and he was clearly unhappy every time. He gave us the same answer. Again.

"I can't tell you why. I can't explain it. I'll know what I want when I see it. This isn't it. Come back when you have something worthwhile to show me."

He stood up and left the room. We all just looked at each other and sighed. Then we went back to the drawing board and started over. Again.

The vast majority of my commanders and other bosses I've had in the Air Force have been excellent — easily more than 90 percent fall in that category. Many were truly remarkable men and women. I've been extremely fortunate to have them as examples of outstanding leadership, integrity, and character. Yet, there have been those who came up short. Two of them stand out as clear examples of leadership failure.

In 1984, shortly after my divorce from Carol, I left March Air Force Base and began my Air Staff Training (ASTRA) tour at the Pentagon. The ASTRA program was designed to give promising mid-level captains at the five- to six-year point an introduction as to how decisions are made at the highest levels of the Air Force. It was a highly selective assignment and I was indeed fortunate to have been chosen. I was grateful for this opportunity.

The Air Force assigned me to a colonel attached to the Joint Staff as a liaison officer from Military Airlift Command (the forerunner to AMC). He was a one-man shop and he needed someone as an assistant to help take care of business, especially while he was away. It certainly sounded interesting and I was excited to get started when I arrived.

What I discovered was an officer who was lacking any sense of integrity or motivation, apart from what served his purposes. He was the consummate "good ole boy." He was great at glad-handing and had a large number of friends and colleagues with whom he dealt. Having a network is a good thing. Using that network to go around the system, exchange favors, and skirt regulations is not good. If there was a decision between a legitimate way to accomplish a task or a backdoor "scratch my back and I'll scratch yours" way to do it, he would invariably choose the latter.

I never saw him do anything illegal. What I did see was the routine exchange of favors outside the system to "make things happen." He was proud of this, too. He would regularly caution me, "don't tell anyone about this, but …" He even tried to get me to enlist my ASTRA friends at the Pentagon to come to his house one weekend to build a hot tub for him (for free). He was possibly the worst example of leadership integrity I've ever seen. What made it even more uncomfortable was that I was the sole witness to all the stuff he was doing.

Along with this, he had been divorced multiple times, due to his infidelity. He was proud of that. He told me how his children described him as having the "morals of an alley cat." In the era before cell phones, he would direct me to lie to his girlfriends about where he was and what he was doing when they called our office looking for him. Since I had just gone through my own divorce where my wife cheated on me, this situation was disappointing, to say the least. I felt like I needed to take a shower every day after I came home from work.

I learned a lot from watching this colonel, although I'm sure it was not what he expected me to learn. Through his unprincipled example, I learned the corrosive effect of working for a leader who lacks integrity. I saw how his behavior undermined his authority and destroyed whatever respect I might have had for him. I vowed never to be "that guy." The good news was that my second six months as an ASTRA officer were outstanding. I worked in an Air Force headquarters division with some great officers, making my Pentagon tour a highly rewarding and fun experience.

My second example of poor leadership was the SAC colonel I described at the very beginning of this chapter. He was a career staff officer, specializing in personnel activities. His entire focus was on looking good, making sure his bosses saw him as an expert. While all of us naturally want to appear competent, his emphasis was an obsession.

He was afraid one of the generals might call him and want information he wouldn't be able to provide instantly. As a result, he expected those of us who worked for him to be available to answer his questions immediately. He wanted someone from our section always ready to pick up the phone. He required us to answer it before it rang a third time. If we didn't have the answer he wanted immediately at our fingertips, that was considered a black mark against us. I was struck by what a fearful existence this man lived.

In the fall of 1988, we in the personnel directorate were asked to brief the SAC staff about our programs and issues. This was an annual event for all directorates and most of our personnel briefings were relatively routine. The one contentious area was the one I was responsible for: officer assignments. Everyone had a stake in the assignment process and all the SAC generals had distinct opinions about how we should do our jobs. The colonel rightfully understood that the officer assignments briefing, which I presented with a colleague of mine, was likely to be the most problematic of the one-hour event.

Rather than allow us to build an informative briefing we could hone as a team, and trust we could field questions, the colonel wanted to create a new and exciting way of showing who we were and what we did to support SAC. Great idea, but he was completely unable to express what he wanted. He had a binary reaction: yes, I like it or no, I don't like it. No further explanation.

The problem was that his response was always "no." No other feedback, just "No, I don't like it." His entire perspective was fear-based. He was deathly afraid of looking bad in front of the SAC commander and the other directorate chiefs. Because of this, he was paralyzed. He was unable to make a decision. His inability to look at a situation as anything other than a threat to him also caused him to lash out in anger when he was frustrated.

Watching a senior officer be so afraid of failure was disheartening. He was unable to act effectively. It was nearly impossible for me to generate any respect for him, apart from the sense of duty I had as an Air Force officer. I wanted to succeed because of the people whose lives I affected, and I always did my best, but I was not motivated by a sense of loyalty to my boss. It was sad.

In the end, our briefing to the SAC senior staff was a complete non-event. We ended up giving a presentation that was nearly identical to what we created as our first draft. We never did find anything the colonel liked. We simply ran out of time to create any more trial balloons for him to shoot down.

The SAC senior staff seemed to like what we showed them that day. It was well received and generated a few questions from them. We answered the questions with no problems. Nothing controversial or contentious. The briefing ended, the SAC commander thanked us, and then he and his staff went on to more important business after we left the conference room.

The colonel remained at SAC headquarters for another year and then retired. He had been hoping to get promoted to brigadier general, but it didn't happen. I'd like to think that SAC senior leadership saw him for what he was — afraid and obsessed with how others viewed him.

I learned a great deal from the colonel, though. I saw how having a fearful, "careerist" mentality can completely undermine a leader's moral authority. This type of attitude demonstrates a lack of integrity and a lack of concern for the people or the mission of an organization. His attitude also showed me how easy it was to see through his behavior. It was impossible for him to hide it.

This experience also reinforced my desire to never be perceived as that type of leader. While I always intended to behave properly and lead with honest motives, watching my boss at SAC showed me that I never wanted to even be thought of as behaving otherwise. The mere perception of impropriety was almost as harmful as actual bad behavior. I was not going to let my actions as a leader be driven by a small-minded, careerist mentality. The respect of my people and my colleagues was far more important than getting that next promotion.

Chapter 23

Bad Decisions

General George Armstrong Custer, who led his men into an ambush at the Battle of the Little Bighorn in 1876. (U.S. government)

JoAnn looked at me and leaned in to say something.

"Those two are having an affair."

I about choked. We were watching Emily's little league baseball game. JoAnn was referring to a maintenance officer who was a major and one of four squadron commanders in my group. The major was talking to his squadron chief of administration, a technical sergeant. She was single and worked directly for him. The major was married with two children.

I looked at JoAnn, startled.

"What do you want me to do with *that* little piece of information?" I asked.

"Nothing special," she said. "I just thought you should know."

Among the many things I appreciate about my wife are her perception and her intuition. She picks up on social cues much faster than I do — it's not even close. She has provided me with her insight, but she understood as the commander or division chief or whatever role I occupied, I had to weigh many different factors when making decisions. This was especially true when my decisions affected the people I lead. Her advice was given freely, and she knew I appreciated it. She also knew I had to have complete freedom to use my best judgment, even if that meant doing what was contrary to her opinion. Almost always, though, her intuition was spot on.

It wasn't long after the incident on the baseball field I decided I wanted feedback on how my group was doing. I had been commander for six months and I wanted to know what was working and what needed to change. At that point in my command, my airmen would have formed opinions about how things were going, and there would still be plenty of time left in my tour to make any changes to improve what wasn't going well. I wanted to hear what they thought, especially if they had any suggestions to improve things.

Robins Air Force Base was large enough to have a team of airmen who were expert at conducting Climate Assessment Surveys. These surveys were carefully crafted to provide information to commanders, like me, who wanted to know where to improve. One of the basic premises for the survey was that it was anonymous, and the results would not be used as part of an officer's evaluation. In other words, if the results showed there was a morale problem in a unit, I could not use that information to punish that unit's commander or any supervisors in the chain of command. I understood and fully supported those ground rules.

What I found was a wide discrepancy between the four squadrons in my group. Three of the squadrons came back with strong indications of high morale and respect for squadron leadership — this was great news and not unexpected. I was also pleased to see the feedback directed at my performance was positive, with the few critiques I received revolving around unintended consequences of some policies I had initiated. I was glad to know about their concerns and worked to correct the situation after I found out.

Unfortunately, the climate survey showed one of my maintenance squadrons had low morale and concerns with how the commander treated people. The difference between that squadron and my other three squadrons was dramatic.

I requested all my squadron commanders meet with me individually to go over the results of the climate survey for their unit. Three of them were pleased to know things were going well and were eager to learn how they might be able to improve. When I met with my maintenance squadron commander, the conversation was a bit different. I began by emphasizing this survey was a snapshot in time and he had an opportunity to improve on areas of concern. I also stressed none of this would be incorporated into his officer performance report and he still had every chance to build on what he learned from the survey to make his squadron the best in the group.

After I went through the results, the major became very defensive. He made it clear he didn't put much faith in surveys like this and pointed to his unit's performance metrics as proof of what a great job he was doing. The fact was his unit had met or exceeded mission-ready goals, and I rightfully gave him credit for that. I also knew his unit had a much higher share of experienced, motivated sergeants and senior airmen than a typical maintenance squadron. These men and women would perform well regardless of who was in charge.

I explained to the major that morale issues often show up before performance drops. I asked him to consider taking this well-meaning feedback to heart and adjust his own style of leadership to be more appreciative of his troops. I may as well have been talking to the wall. The major was very "old school," working his way through the enlisted ranks before becoming an officer. He had about as much time in the Air Force as I did at that point. I could tell by his body language he couldn't wait for this "useless" meeting to be over.

Months later, morale issues began to surface. His squadron was the only unit in my group that had its members get arrested for Driving Under the Influence (DUI) of alcohol. Apart from the serious legal issues and potentially tragic safety consequences for the individuals involved, this had a big impact within my group. Because I emphasized safety as a top priority in my group, I offered everyone one Friday off each month if we met all our operational and training goals. We also had to have zero DUIs within the group. My emphasis on this was deliberate. I had seen the terrible consequences of drunk driving during my career and I wanted to do all I could to prevent problems in my group. Meeting our flying goals was tough, but we always achieved them, despite routinely flying missions on weekends and regularly deploying on missions in the Pacific, Europe, Asia, and the Middle East.

It was the DUIs that would trip us up. For several months in a row, a different member of this major's squadron would be arrested for DUI. And each month, I would take away the opportunity for the group to enjoy a well-deserved "extra" day off. I began asking questions of the major and his senior staff individually. What was causing this? The peer pressure from the rest of the group had to be enormous. I began to get answers, and they weren't good.

I've never subscribed to the theory that people who work for me had to adhere to my leadership style. All of us are different, and there are many successful leaders who have very different styles than I do. Clearly, they're doing what works for them, and I wouldn't dream of interfering in their success. Like my commanders had done for me earlier in my career, I wanted to give my squadron leaders the flexibility to lead their organizations in a way that suits them best.

There's a difference between style and values, though. When one of my officers or airmen doesn't adhere to our shared Air Force values and doesn't support my goals as their commander, that is a huge issue. That's what was happening here. I insisted on my commanders treating their people with respect and dignity, and I did my best to lead by example. After listening to feedback from several of the senior NCOs, it was clear the major relied heavily on intimidation and ridicule to motivate his people. One incident stuck out: he had made fun of his second-in-command, a young lieutenant, in front of his assembled squadron. I heard the major thought this was a good way to keep the lieutenant in line. But I was appalled he would undermine the authority of one of his officers.

When I found out, I directed the major to come see me in my office that afternoon. I intended to let him know his "leadership style" was unacceptable in my group and he needed to change ASAP. It was clear his intimidation tactics were a root cause of the DUIs within his group. Fear and a lack of respect will cause people to do self-damaging things to draw attention to themselves and their situation. This was the same major who had publicly made fun of the senior master sergeant who stuttered during a presentation. This guy was a problem and my patience had run out.

Before my meeting with the major, I needed to attend a base-wide ceremony for noncommissioned officers who had just been selected for promotion to master sergeant. This was a huge deal, because becoming a master sergeant meant the NCO had achieved the status of a senior noncommissioned officer. Competition was intense for promotion to this rank and it indicated a high skill level and an intense dedication to the Air Force for those who achieved it. I was very proud of all the men and women in my group who had been promoted and my presence at the ceremony was important to them and to me.

At the ceremony, it was usually family members (spouses and children) who pinned the new rank on their recently promoted master sergeants. There were four of us (colonels) on stage representing our groups. We were there to congratulate all promotees, especially those from our group. We were also there to present the new rank to those members of our group who were single or whose family members couldn't make the ceremony. When it came time for the unmarried chief of administration in my maintenance squadron to receive her stripes, the major stepped on stage to present her with them. My jaw dropped. This was the same couple JoAnn had warned me about months earlier on that baseball field. Their behavior was in full display and completely out of line.

When I returned to my office after the ceremony, I called the major and told him to see me immediately. I then asked my deputy to come to my office when the major arrived. I was going to give the major a direct order and I wanted a senior-ranking witness. I had enough and I was going to put an end to this right now.

When the major arrived, I called my deputy in and asked him to shut the door. I read the major the riot act. I told him his leadership style was completely unacceptable in my group and he was having a negative impact on the people he was supposed to be leading. I told him I was done trying to counsel him — I clearly wasn't having any effect. I was removing him from command, effective at the end of the week. I needed a couple of days to find a replacement.

I also told him I would find a short-term position for him on base suitable for a major with his experience. Despite his leadership failure, the major was technically very adept and the Air Logistics Center at Robins was always short-handed on officers with maintenance experience, even if they were only available on a temporary basis. I informed the major he would continue to report to me through the end of the lieutenant colonel promotion board in a couple of months — this was his primary zone selection board. I did this so I could hold him accountable for his behavior. I also advised him he needed to contact the Air Force Personnel Center and line up another job someplace else — staying at Robins wasn't a good option.

Finally, I looked the major right in the eyes and asked him why he was on stage with his chief of administration at the promotion ceremony. Did he not notice that the only people on stage with the promotees were loved ones or their group commander?

He gave a lame excuse, claiming he didn't know this was a problem. He was "just trying to be supportive of one of his troops." He said it was all a misunderstanding.

I asked him point blank: "Are you having an affair with her?"

"No, sir. No, sir," he stammered.

"Then I am giving you a direct order, in front of Colonel Stark as a witness. So there will be no misunderstanding about what I'm telling you to do, you are to have no contact with the sergeant from this point forward. In the few days you have left as commander, if you need to conduct official business with her, you will only do so in your squadron building with someone else present. Always. If you don't adhere to what I'm telling you, to the letter, you will be in violation of my orders and I will react accordingly. Do you understand everything I've told you today?"

"Yes, sir." He looked down.

"You're dismissed," I said bluntly.

He gave a half-hearted salute and shuffled out of my office. I was glad to see him go.

The topic of marital infidelity is a sensitive one in the military. Adultery is not punishable under the Uniform Code of Military Justice (UCMJ); however, Article 134 of the UCMJ prohibits conduct which brings discredit upon the armed forces or conduct which is prejudicial to good order and discipline. Article 134 is a "catch all" disciplinary action, designed to allow commanders the leeway to discipline people for anything they deem hurts morale and/or the performance of the unit.

I've never seen my role as enforcer of moral standards. Morality is highly individual, and it's not up to me to decide what's right and what's wrong. On the other hand, an important role I had as an officer and leader was to insure I and all members of my unit supported the core values of the Air Force: Integrity first, Service before self, and Excellence in all we do. I had no problem disciplining members who willfully fell short.

Being unfaithful to a spouse shows a lack of integrity. It calls into question whether that person can be trusted and where their loyalties really lie. This is especially a problem in a close-knit Air Force unit, such as a squadron. We all knew each other and looked after one another, including our spouses. We socialized regularly and we were friends. I never wanted to be put in a situation where I was covering up for someone else's bad behavior. It happened once to me early in my career as a young captain and I vowed never to allow myself to be put in that position again.

Once I assumed a squadron leadership role as the Operations Officer of the 344th Air Refueling Squadron in North Carolina in early 1993, I felt I had the responsibility to call out this behavior to the individuals involved if I ever saw it occurring. Even though I didn't seek out offenders, sometimes their behavior was apparent to anyone who saw them. Within months of my taking over this new position, I deployed to Al Dhafra Air Base in the United Arab Emirates for the first time. The aircrews and maintenance crews were from my squadron and our sister KC-10 squadron from Seymour Johnson AFB, the 911th.

Shortly after our arrival, I got word from several sources that one of the 911th pilots was spending all his spare time with a female maintenance troop. He was married with children; she was single. Even though he wasn't in my squadron back home, I knew him and his wife. I pulled him aside the first chance I got.

"I hear you're hanging around Airman (Smith) a whole lot. What's going on with you two?"

"Uhhh … nothing, sir."

"Let me make this clear. I've heard from several people it looks like you're fooling around. Knock it off."

"We're just friends, sir."

"It doesn't matter. Even if what you're saying is true and this is completely innocent, it looks bad. Really bad."

"Sir?"

"I'm telling you right now, if I see or hear about you two spending any time together from now on, I'm sending you home on the next plane out. You can explain to your wife why you were singled out to come home early from the deployment. Do you understand?"

"Yes, sir."

He was shaken up. But he stayed away from the airman and completed his tour without further problem.

For my major maintenance squadron commander, the problem was far greater than infidelity, though. He was apparently having an affair with a woman who worked directly for him, a woman who had just been promoted, largely based on his support. The appearance of favoritism was blinding, even if the promotion was well deserved and everything else was a coincidence. Yet, having no hard evidence and in the face of his denials, the most I could do was remove him from his position of authority.

Until one month later. One of my other squadron commanders and his wife had gone to a movie in Macon, 30 miles away from where we were stationed. While at the movie, they saw the major and the master sergeant on a date. The squadron commander who saw them passed that information on to me. Clearly, the major felt he would be far enough away from home station that he could get away with seeing her.

The major had violated my order and had been caught. One more time, I called him into my office. I also asked Colonel Stark to witness what I was going to say. The major arrived and reported in. As he stood in front of me, his slumped shoulders and worried look showed me he knew exactly why he was there.

"Major, I understand you were at a movie with your former chief of administration. Did you not understand the order I gave you?"

"Sir, we were coordinating activities for our two children. They're on the same basketball team and we're the two coaches. Besides, she's not in my squadron anymore."

This was so much crap and he knew it. He knew I knew it, too.

"Who are you trying to kid? It was a date. We all know it. My order was very specific. You were not to see her under any circumstances, and you violated it."

Pause.

"I'm changing my recommendation for your lieutenant colonel promotion board to Do Not Promote. I've already talked with the 21st Air Force commander and he agrees with my change. You will be passed over for promotion. Based on your time of service, you will be required to retire from the Air Force in a matter of months. Your assignment to Japan will be cancelled. Your Air Force career will be over soon."

Pause.

"You're dismissed."

He turned and left my office. I never saw him again, although his wife's lawyer asked me to provide a written deposition for his divorce trial a few months later. I did.

The major squadron commander and the captain pilot I described above willfully violated informal policy and social norms. When confronted with their behavior, they chose different paths. The captain straightened up and made it through the rest of his deployment without any problem. The major made a bad decision, choosing to disobey my order. He ended up terminating his career through his own misbehavior. In both cases, I decided to give them an opportunity to take responsibility for their own actions. Also, in both cases, while the decisions I made and actions I took were difficult, I never felt conflicted. I felt I was doing the right thing.

Unfortunately, that wasn't always the case. Near the end of my tour as group commander at Robins, I had a chief master sergeant with a serious gambling problem. I wasn't aware of the depth of his problem until it came to my attention he had used his government credit card at automatic teller machines in the Biloxi (Mississippi) casinos. He had driven there over the weekend and evidently lost a lot of money. He wasn't married, so there weren't any family support issues involved. Still, using an Air Force-issued credit card for non-Air Force expenses was a serious violation.

When base leadership found out about this, I found myself under strong peer pressure to make an example of this chief and punish him severely. Chief master sergeants hold the highest Air Force enlisted rank and represent the top 1 percent of the enlisted force. They are always expected to uphold the highest standards. Others saw his flagrant violation of the rules as nearly unforgiveable. I saw the chief's problem as a behavioral issue and not a discipline problem, so I gave him an Article 15 with suspended punishment. I also had a lengthy counselling session with him and directed him to enroll in an addiction treatment program at our base hospital. My decision was unpopular with my colonel friends — they saw this as being too easy on a senior NCO whom I liked. And while I did respect and like the chief, I felt I was doing the fairest thing for him while still recognizing the severity of his violation.

Unfortunately, one month later the chief relapsed. Because I had taken away his Air Force credit card, he chose to "borrow" $500 from the Unit Enlisted Welfare Fund, of which he had gotten himself elected treasurer. This was terribly sad and just too much to forgive. I vacated his Article 15 suspension and executed all punishments I had previously set aside. I also had to decide what to do next. Because this was a second occurrence for a similar violation, I needed to do something substantial. This was way bigger than the chief and me now. I felt I needed to demonstrate to my group that all of us had to abide by the rules, no matter what rank we were. For his own good, I also felt I needed to give the chief a severe wake-up call—something that would get his attention in a big way. I recommended him for a trial by court-martial. It hurt me to do this to a man I respected and admired.

The chief's trial went quickly — it was straight forward, and he didn't dispute any of the facts. He was found guilty and reduced in rank to senior master sergeant. In addition to an immediate drop in pay, he would likely lose more than a hundred thousand dollars over his lifetime in reduced retirement pay. The result was fair, yet it was still sad to see. Interestingly, I received sympathetic responses from my other colonel friends on base. The common reaction was they admired me sticking up for my guy, even though I was going contrary to prevailing opinion. They, too, found it disheartening to see a chief stand trial for an addiction-related offense.

Identifying and correcting inappropriate behavior is a critical role for a leader. It helps individuals to see when they're out-of-line. Whether they're doing it intentionally or not, improper or illegal behavior needs to be corrected. Along with that, it's important to demonstrate to other members of the unit that standards are going to be upheld. Anything less invites discipline problems and other behavioral issues from the unit.

I felt it was also important to demonstrate compassion for individuals. The chief needed a second chance to correct his behavior, along with an opportunity to take advantage of counseling services on base. I'm sure my troops saw that, too. One size doesn't fit all. Sometimes, a leader needs to make an exception to policy. The challenge is knowing when to make that exception.

Finally, a leader can't make these difficult disciplinary decisions if he or she doesn't uphold these same standards. I believed my behavior needed to be above reproach. At the same time, I also felt I could not afford to be "best buddies" with anyone who I commanded — I needed to maintain a little distance in the unfortunate event I had to enforce disciplinary actions, such as with my maintenance squadron commander. My responsibility was to the Air Force and those leaders above me. At the same time my loyalty was also with the men and women under my command. I wanted to be approachable and connect with them as well. I wanted them to succeed and I wanted to do my very best to support their success.

Correcting inappropriate behavior, enforcing discipline, showing compassion, maintaining standards, keeping some distance, and connecting with those under my command was a difficult balancing act. I wouldn't have had it any other way.

PART 4

TRUST

JoAnn and me in Yosemite National Park, 2017

Chapter 24

Facing My Fears

Spoiler alert: My beautiful daughter Emily and me in 1992.
Go Bears!

"Rees 31 Solo, what are your intentions?"

The control tower at Reese Air Force Base needed an answer. They were asking me what I wanted to do next with my T-38. Did I want to set myself up for a long straight-in approach to a full-stop landing? I could tell from the controller's voice this is what he was recommending. Even though it was a moonless night, air traffic control saw exactly what happened. They knew I nearly crashed and killed myself and I must be pretty shaken up. They were right on all counts. And they were giving me an out. I didn't need to do anything more than land the aircraft to successfully complete my night solo ride. It was very tempting to just fly the straight-in and call it a night. This was my last T-38 night flight before moving onto the next training module.

At the ripe old age of 23, though, I knew I was at a decision point in my life. At that moment, I even had doubts about whether I wanted to continue being a pilot. The entire episode had frightened me that much. Still, I knew in my heart that if I didn't try the overhead maneuver again and do it correctly, for the rest of my life I would feel as if I had surrendered to my own fears. As I sped along at 180 MPH, I keyed the microphone to talk with the air traffic controller.

Fast forward 11 years to 1989. I was sitting in the Air Force doctor's office at Offutt Air Force Base near Omaha, Nebraska.

"You'll never be able to father a child. Your sperm count is much too low."

The doctor was talking to me, but I couldn't pay attention after his first sentence. I had feared this for a long time. I suspected this might be the case, and I tried to prepare myself for what could come, but I wasn't ready for what he said.

His words devastated me. I saw the doctor during my lunch break at Strategic Air Command Headquarters and I needed to return to my desk job after my appointment. I was numb. I had to continue even though I wanted to go home and just be with my grief. After I returned to work, I called my fiancée, JoAnn. She knew I had an appointment and wanted to hear what the doctor said. I couldn't voice anything except "I'll tell you about it later." If I even approached the subject, I felt I would lose it. Without me saying anything more, JoAnn knew something was very wrong.

In 1989, having such a low sperm count meant there was very little chance of fathering a child. In vitro fertilization was just beginning, and it was extremely expensive for those who even tried to go that route. At the time I was engaged to JoAnn, who would become my wife (as of this writing we've been married 29 years). We were both 34, and I told her I wanted to have children, as we got more serious about marriage and topics like this came up. JoAnn was a registered nurse, and she asked about whether Carol and I had tried to have children in the three years we were married. I told her yes, we had, but with no success. Any medical tests on either of us? No, we hadn't gotten to that point.

JoAnn knew my medical history, too. I had been born two months premature near the end of 1954. Even then, my mother spent the last month of her pregnancy in the hospital on bed rest because I was half-detached from her placenta. Since I was only at seven months when I was born, my testicles had never descended. My parents tried to correct this when I was an infant, but I became sick when they scheduled the procedure and they cancelled the surgery.

The surgery didn't get rescheduled until I was 7- and 8-years-old — much later than normal. My mother had also taken Diethylstilbestrol (DES), a drug given to pregnant women in the 1950s to prevent complications during pregnancy. Side effects of DES included increased risk of testicular abnormalities, undescended testicles, and development of cysts. The result of all of this was that my genitals, while functioning, were underdeveloped.

JoAnn knew it also might mean I have a low sperm count. She encouraged me to see a doctor, so we would know what the situation was, one way or another. And the news, as I feared, was the worst. The test results showed my sperm count was 200,000. A normal, healthy male has a count in the tens of millions.

After the long afternoon ended, I left work and drove to JoAnn's house where she lived with her 10-year-old son Justin. Justin was gone when I got there. I don't recall the specifics, but I'm sure she arranged for him to be away. When she met me at the door, I did something she had never seen me do before. I burst into tears.

After I composed myself enough to talk to her, I told her all about what happened. I described how I had always wanted to be a father just like my dad. I shared how I always imagined two or three children of my own who I could love and raise and who would know I cared for them and protected them. I told her how I wanted children who loved and respected me, just as I had loved and respected my father. I told her how this dream had just been ripped from me. I didn't know what to do, much less deal with a future far different from the one I had always envisioned.

JoAnn lovingly reassured me we would get through this together. This was an enormous relief. All afternoon I had nursed an unfounded fear she wouldn't want to marry someone who was less than fully a man and who couldn't provide her with another child. JoAnn was born to be a Mom. She's extremely smart, capable, and funny, and had fashioned a career of her own as an RN, but her love in life was children.

She already had an amazing son, but it was clear when we had our "do you want any more children" talk, she was enthusiastically all in. And now, in my moment of extreme vulnerability, she could not have been more loving, more understanding, or more beautiful. She told me how much she loved me and was looking forward to being my wife. She also told me this doctor's prognosis was far from the last word on this and she would be with me every step of the way, regardless of what we decided to do. For her amazing, unconditional love, I will always be profoundly grateful.

Chapter 25

Home for Christmas

(Alpha Stock Images)

Perhaps the most disheartening incident regarding my Mom's alcoholism was Christmas, 1986. At the time, I was a KC-10 instructor pilot at Barksdale Air Force Base outside of Shreveport, Louisiana. Carol and I had been divorced two years and two assignments ago. I had a new girlfriend, Melanie. She lived in San Jose, near where I grew up. Mutual friends introduced us to each other earlier in 1986. Mom and Dad had moved back to our old house in Los Altos after Dad retired from Lockheed at the beginning of the year.

During the fall of 1986, I came up with what I considered a clever idea for a "morale trip" over Christmas. My crew and I would plan and fly a KC-10 mission from Barksdale headed westbound, landing at Mather AFB near Sacramento, California. We would load up the plane with single airmen who had family on the West Coast. My idea was that we would provide transportation for them to California, so they could spend Christmas with family and friends instead of being alone and away from home. We would fly a training mission both coming and going, so we would use the plane effectively without wasting the squadron's flying funds.

I pitched my idea to my squadron commander and then we both went to the wing commander. The two of them loved it. In fact, they added an eastbound flight, too. Everyone on the flights, both crews and the passengers, were enthusiastic volunteers. These flights needed a great deal of planning and preparation, but I was happy to spearhead the effort because it meant I would spend Christmas with my girlfriend and my family, including my brothers and sister, for the first time in many years.

The day came, and my crew and I flew the refueling mission, landing at Mather AFB in mid-afternoon. Once my crew and I got our KC-10 bedded down, we reconfirmed our rendezvous time a week from then and ensured our contact information was correct in case we needed to return to base suddenly. We wished each other a Merry Christmas and then parted ways. I was heading home.

It was exhilarating, and it was great to see Melanie — she had gotten the day off work and met me in base operations. She drove us the two hours straight to my parents' home, the house where I grew up, so I could say hi to Mom and Dad and drop off my stuff. We arrived home and the front door was open. I walked in, but nobody was home. They knew when I would arrive, and I was right on time (as usual). There was no note or anything. Something felt very wrong.

Melanie and I waited at home for more than an hour. Finally, Dad walked in the door. He had just delivered Mom to rehab. Again. Her drinking had gotten so bad she once again checked herself in. To say I was disappointed would be a gross understatement. I felt like someone had kicked me in the gut. Here I made this special effort to be with them — the first time I had been able to spend the holidays with family for years — and Mom was in such bad shape she would be away for Christmas with yet another trip to rehab. Damn it. I was angry at her for screwing things up again with her obsessive drinking.

I felt sorry for Dad, too. He had to deal with this situation all the time. I hated feeling sorry for Dad. It didn't seem right to feel sorry for a man like him. At the same time, a part of me felt relieved. At least we wouldn't have to be dealing with my Mom's drinking this Christmas because she would be in a treatment center. It felt like cold comfort, but at least it was something. I don't remember feeling concerned about Mom. I had seen this play out so many times before, my expectations were close to zero, even though I never lost hope "this might be the time." Unfortunately, this all transpired in front of Melanie. This was embarrassing even though she already knew the situation with my Mom.

Making things worse, though, was the situation with my older brother Dave. Dave has always been smart, loving, and an extraordinarily talented and creative musician. Besides working as a highly successful technical recruiter, his first love is music. The founder of an extremely popular country swing band in Austin, Texas, Dave has led the Cornell Hurd Band since its inception in the 1970s through today. I could not be prouder of my oldest brother, who has raised two wonderful sons under some trying circumstances.

In December 1986, Dave was going downhill quickly — he was a cocaine addict. He and his first marriage were disintegrating before our eyes on an almost daily basis. I would get calls in Louisiana from my parents or my sister Caroline or brother Drew about Dave. While I wanted to know what was going on, I dreaded those calls because I felt so helpless. More than that, though, I worried the next call would tell me he was dead or in jail. Finally, just before the Christmas holidays, things came to a head. Dad, with some loving and sober friends of Dave, convinced him to go to a drug rehabilitation center in Florida — far away from his environment and contacts in California.

A couple of days before I made my trip to California, Dave and a friend of his got on a plane to Tampa, where Dave checked himself in for treatment. Even though Dave was entering rehab just like Mom had done so many times before, this felt different. In Dave's case, he needed a rescue, a way out. He needed to break the cycle, or his addiction would have killed him. His going to rehab was a relief, and I was happy when he made that decision.

So, there we were. I had just come home and my Mom and my much loved and admired oldest brother Dave were in rehabilitation centers. When I wasn't with Melanie or some of my high school or college friends still living in the Bay Area, I spent much of my Christmas visiting Mom at the treatment center or talking with Dave on the phone. We also gathered as a family: Dad, Caroline, Drew, and I.

We spent one entire day cleaning things up with Dave. His wife Kathy had left him, and their home was a complete disaster. We rented a trash container and threw half of what they owned in it or took their things to the dump ourselves. We took salvageable items to a rented storage unit for whenever Dave wanted to deal with it. Thank God Dad was there and strong as always.

This was the most depressing Christmas I had ever experienced. Between the rehab visits and phone calls, the day-long cleanup of Dave's place, and the mostly joyless Christmas Day gathering, I was glad to go back to the Air Force and my flying job in Louisiana when it was all done. Back to normalcy and stability. I want to add, despite things not working out for us, I will always appreciate my then-girlfriend Melanie for all her support during that miserable Christmas. It meant a great deal.

I'm happy to add a postscript before leaving this chapter. My amazing brother David Cornell Hurd is doing tremendously, and I could not be prouder of him. He has been sober for the last 32 years — ever since he checked himself into rehab in 1986. Of all the many things about my brother that make me proud, I am most proud of his sobriety and the support and love he generously gives to so many people while creating a wonderful life for himself and his family. He has raised two wonderful sons, Vance and Casey, and he has established himself as the leader of one of Austin's premier country swing bands, The Cornell Hurd Band. It still plays nationally and internationally.

I even saw the band in 2005 and 2006 when they headlined country music festivals in France and Switzerland — I was stationed in Belgium at the time. And while I'm very proud of my brother's musical and leadership abilities, I'm most impressed with his poise and eloquence. I witnessed European media representatives interview him in 2005 and 2006, a time when U.S. foreign policy was quite unpopular in Europe because of the Iraq War. Dave fielded difficult questions in a gracious and appreciative manner, all the while representing country music and the United States very well. No one I know could have done any better. He was magnificent. I am so grateful to have him as my older brother.

Chapter 26

JoAnn

JoAnn and me at an Air Force Ball in 1995

I listened to my answering machine recording from New Beginnings, the video dating service I had just joined an hour earlier. The receptionist, the young woman who had interviewed me as part of the check-in process, had called and left a message while I was driving home. "There's a woman who just saw your video — she walked in right after you left. She wants to meet you. Her name is JoAnn." *"Wow,"* I thought. *"This place works really well."* I would find out soon it worked perfectly.

I moved to Omaha in January 1988 — my relocation from Louisiana to Nebraska was the result of a new assignment. Instead of being a KC-10 instructor pilot, I was now assigned to Strategic Air Command (SAC) headquarters at Offutt Air Force Base. I would be a personnel officer, helping make assignments and assignment policy for pilots and navigators assigned to SAC. SAC had about 100,000 people — it was huge. The Air Force considered my new assignment a good career move, because it provided me the opportunity to learn about the Air Force personnel business. The Air Force viewed being knowledgeable about assignments and career progression as an area that helped prepare an officer for command. Still, I wasn't overly thrilled to be removed from flying and move due north into the frozen reaches of the Midwest. While I realized things were better in Omaha than Upper Michigan, this California boy remembered all too well the bitterly cold winters on the shores of Lake Superior.

I had been divorced for almost four years at that point. By the time I got my assignment to Omaha, Melanie and I had decided to go our separate ways. I was on my own when I arrived in Nebraska. After six months in my new job in the nearly all-male SAC HQ, I had gone nowhere in my social life. The few dates I had were, by mutual consent, nothing either party wanted to follow up on. My friends at work were all married. By that time, the Air Force had promoted me to major, I was 33-years-old, and virtually everyone my age or even close to my age was married. None of their spouses knew any single women. At least, that's what they told me, and I chose to believe them. So, not only did I not know any women to go out with, my buddies at work were married and their social lives understandably revolved around their families. The whole situation was a bridge to nowhere for my social life.

The good news, though, was that my younger brother Kevin, an Air Force navigator in Offutt's RC-135 reconnaissance squadron, was also stationed at Offutt. He was 31 and he wasn't dating anyone, either. I loved hanging out with Kevin when he wasn't on one of his frequent deployments to Okinawa, England, or Greece. We typically would get together after work on Friday and grab a bite to eat. There was zero planning beyond the decision to meet and whose car we'd take.

We literally would drive down the main drag in Bellevue (the town right next to the base) and one of us would point to a restaurant and say, "Let's go there." So we would. After dinner we'd drive to the nearby movie complex and get two tickets for whatever film was playing next — it didn't matter what it was. That's how we got to see some classically bad movies. I freely admit our extreme "go with the flow" behavior was completely ridiculous. And I loved it.

As great as hanging out with Kevin was, I wanted to have a social life outside of random restaurants and bad movies with my brother. One morning, as I was shaving, I heard an ad on the radio for a place called "New Beginnings." It was a video dating service. I stopped and wrote down the number.

"My God, this seems pretty desperate," I remember thinking. Immediately after, I also remember thinking, *"Well, I am pretty desperate. Why not?"*

Having awakened to my desperation, I visited the New Beginnings offices way across town that Saturday. I called ahead and made an appointment, which is when I found out I needed to show them my most recent tax return to confirm I was indeed single. Clever. I also discovered there was a membership fee, which they only charged the men.

While I balked a little at the "unfairness" of gender-based membership fees, my rationalization process was full-steam ahead, so nothing was going to stop me. I signed up for a one-year membership. As I recall that was the shortest and least expensive membership plan available. I also figured if things weren't progressing after one year at this place, it probably wasn't for me.

The next step was to fill out a one-page information form and attach a small photo of myself (I had brought a photo, too, per their instructions). Once I finished with the preliminaries, I went into the filming room and submitted to a 15-minute interview with the attractive receptionist. She asked me a series of questions, some of which were loosely based on what I had written on my form. After that, my membership was complete.

I could have looked at the "book of women" (the one-sheet summaries written by the women who were members), but by that point I was a little overwhelmed. I felt it would be better if I went home and came back the next day for a fresh look at the situation. I got in my car and drove the 30-minute ride home. By the time I arrived, there was a message on my answering machine. It was New Beginnings. There was a woman who had seen my video, and she wanted to meet me. Her name was JoAnn.

We must have just missed each other at the offices. The next step was for me to go back to New Beginnings and look at JoAnn's video. If I was interested, the office would give me her phone number and I would call and make a date. I was excited I had someone interested in me after being a member for an entire half hour. I went back to New Beginnings, looked at her video and immediately decided I wanted to meet this attractive, charming woman. I called her that evening. We went on a date later that week, and we married in November of the following year. In between a lot of wonderful happened.

JoAnn is one of the most fun and intelligent women I know, and she's just as pretty now as when I met her close to 30 years ago. She's interesting and bright and has a huge heart. I was very attracted to her the moment we met. The best decision I ever made in my life was asking her to marry me and I'm grateful every day she agreed to be my wife. Amen. Hallelujah.

Chapter 27

Learning to Trust

*Me waving out of my KC-135 cockpit after my last Air Force flight
in June 2001. I trusted the system to take care of us and had recently learned
I was getting an amazing follow-on assignment to Germany. (U.S. Air Force)*

The words still rang in my ears. "With your low sperm count, you'll
never be able to father a child."

"What do I do next?" I thought.

The day after I saw the Air Force doctor, I made an appointment to see
a specialist at the University of Nebraska at Omaha. I wanted to explore as
many alternatives as I could. We ran tests, and I took different medications
attempting to increase my sperm count. Within a month or two, I had
exploratory surgery to see what my plumbing was like, which is when the
doctor discovered "pre-cancerous cells" on my testicle, adding another
unfortunate and painful twist to this situation. The process continued to go

nowhere. After each time a doctor would say "there's nothing we can do for you," I insisted on getting a recommendation for another doctor or clinic specializing in fertility.

After months and months of this, seeing four different doctors who all came to the same conclusion, JoAnn, Justin, and I had to move because I was being reassigned in the summer of 1990 to attend the Army Command and General Staff College (CGSC) at Fort Leavenworth, Kansas. CGSC is where the best Army majors go for one year of focused professional development. As an Air Force officer, I was something of a "foreign exchange student" from one of the other military services. The Air Force also considered it a real plus to get selected for this level of advanced education. In the meantime, JoAnn and I were married in November of 1989 in Omaha in a beautiful, family-only ceremony with parents, brothers, and sisters.

I've had to trust throughout my married life with JoAnn. I've had to trust JoAnn would take care of our family and home when I had to deploy overseas. I've had to trust Justin and Emily would be taken care of as they went off to college. And JoAnn has had to trust me to act in a way that would make her proud while I've travelled away from home. All of this is normal and pretty much in due course. There have been times, though, when my (or our) trust has been challenged, particularly when decisions we made required us to just have the faith to know everything will turn out all right.

One example of this was when I was talking with my bosses and the Air Mobility Command (AMC) colonel assignments chief as I was coming up on reassignment after my tour as commander of the 19th Air Refueling Group was ending in 2001. AMC handles colonel assignments on a case-by-case basis because of the low number of colonels in the Air Force and the specific expertise and high level of responsibility required in each colonel-designated position. As I approached the end of my tour, the generals I talked with were near-unanimous in their recommendation I needed to go to Air Force headquarters in Washington for my post-command assignment.

While I appreciated their input, going back to DC to work in an office in the bowels of the Pentagon just didn't feel good. JoAnn didn't like the idea, either, since Emily was turning 10 and about to enter 5th grade. We wanted something more family-friendly. We also wanted to go someplace fun. We had dutifully moved where the Air Force had sent us all these years and we wanted to live somewhere special. Someplace we wouldn't normally go if we weren't in the military. We went to Europe on vacation as a family in the summer of 2000 and we fell in love with the idea of being stationed in Germany where the Air Force had thousands of military members living.

The problem was that all the senior officers I spoke to didn't know of any "tanker colonel" jobs there. Since the vast majority of tankers were stationed in the U.S., and all but a few tanker-related headquarters jobs were here, too, my prospects for an overseas assignment looked nearly impossible. Regardless, I reached out to all my general officer contacts in Europe and friends of mine in assignments-related jobs in the U.S. to let them know my desires.

The response was always the same: "You've done a great job with the 19th and I'd love to help you. In fact, I have this job over here at XYZ Air Force Base (or the Pentagon) if you're interested. Other than that, I've got nothing. You know there are no tanker jobs in Germany, don't you?" JoAnn, Emily, and I stopped pushing to make this happen and just let God line up the perfect assignment for us. We needed to trust the Universe to make it happen.

It wasn't two weeks after we stopped pushing and started allowing that I got a call from General Williams, my two-star boss in New Jersey.

"Bruce, have I got news for you. General Robertson (the four-star Air Mobility Command commander) wants to assign you to the Chief of Programs and Mobility job at European Command (EUCOM) in Stuttgart, Germany. Are you interested?"

To take the call, I had been pulled away from the 99th squadron debrief room where I was sharing a beer with some of my crew after we completed a training flight that Friday afternoon. It took me a second to absorb what he said. This was exactly what I wanted. After I recovered, I thanked General Williams and said I definitely wanted the job. I must have repeated that statement at least three or four times. I wanted to be sure there was no uncertainty.

Once I got off the phone with the general, I called JoAnn on her cell phone — she was with her sister in Orlando, Florida. I had to moderate my emotions. It might not have looked good to have the colonel doing the happy dance around the squadron ready room. JoAnn, on the other hand, didn't hold back. She was crying tears of excitement and joy.

It turned out it wasn't the generals I had been talking with who initiated and coordinated my assignment to Germany. It was a lieutenant colonel at Air Mobility Command headquarters: Rich Johnston. Rich was the chief of colonel assignments. He had the high visibility and often thankless job of arranging assignments for colonels who had tanker or airlift backgrounds, like me. His job often involved having to talk with colonels regarding potential assignments. Unfortunately, many of my colonel colleagues liked to throw their weight around when dealing with someone whom they outranked. I'm sure Rich had to become adept at deflecting questions and not letting verbal abuse get to him.

As a colonel in a group command position, I talked with Rich on a variety of issues — not just my assignment. I always treated him with respect and let him know how much I and the rest of AMC appreciated the job he was doing. As part of our conversations, I had let him know about my desires. I didn't lay any expectations on him regarding what he could or should do for me. It was just a data point for him to consider. I had no idea he had inputs into that EUCOM position — I didn't even know the position existed.

Beyond reinforcing the wisdom of trusting, there's another lesson here: Treat everyone with respect and consideration. It's just an uplifting way of dealing with people, regardless of anything they might do for me. Apart from that, there may come a time when colleagues can really help, like recommending me for a great job exactly where I want to go.

As a postscript, this assignment led to follow-on assignments at the Defense Language Institute in Monterey, California (to learn French) and a two-year tour working for the U.S. Ambassador in Brussels, Belgium, where

I finished up in the Air Force. Besides making great friends, I enjoyed my jobs tremendously, and the locations could not have been better. JoAnn, Emily, and I all agree that Germany, Monterey, and Belgium were the absolute best places we were ever stationed during my Air Force career.

Chapter 28

Having Faith

My wonderful bonus son Justin and beautiful daughter-in-law Jeanette at their wedding in 2007.

"The chances you will have a baby are slim — maybe 10 percent at most. There just aren't many sperm to work with; although the ones you have are healthy. Even with what we can do, it will be difficult and expensive. It will cost more than $10,000 for one shot at this."

The lead doctor at the Reproductive Resources Center (RRC) in Kansas City was sitting across the table from JoAnn and me and he was giving us his view of the situation.

JoAnn and I looked at each other. We both knew what the other was thinking.

"Of course. Yes. We want to try. What's the next step?"

Once the three of us arrived in Kansas in the summer of 1990, JoAnn and I contacted the RRC in Kansas City. The last doctor I saw in Omaha referred us to them when I pressed him to send me somewhere else where they might help me. This was the first time we had seen a doctor at a facility where they did nothing but assist couples who were having difficulty conceiving children.

The first thing I remember seeing as I entered the RRC offices was a large bulletin board filled with pictures of happy little children. These were all the babies they had helped to conceive. For the first time since we had started this ordeal a year earlier, my heart began to sing when I thought maybe, just maybe they could help me father a child.

After weeks of tests and analysis, the doctor gave us his perspective. The chances were small, and it would be expensive. In 1990, $10,000 was a lot of money, especially on an Air Force major's salary. Since the military medical system didn't cover in vitro fertilization — they considered it "experimental" — all expenses would have to be paid by us. JoAnn was just starting to work part-time, since she had to give up her well-paying, established nursing position in Omaha for us to move to Leavenworth. The doctor closed by saying, "If you want to give it a try, we're willing to work with you. Every couple deserves a chance."

Before I go on further, I want to talk about my stepson Justin. Justin was my "first" child and has developed into an amazing, wonderful man with a beautiful, accomplished wife and two fantastic children of his own. As with many step-relationships, there was a tentative beginning between us as we got to know each other. However, over time, we grew to appreciate and love each other.

Justin is remarkable in so many ways. He is an excellent athlete — he was on the basketball, baseball, and golf teams at his high schools and did quite well. I say "schools" because Justin went to four different high schools, one for each year we were in North Carolina, California, Alabama,

178

and Virginia from 1993 to 1997. Justin had the misfortune of going to high school right when the Air Force assigned me to command a squadron for one year, followed by attendance at the Air War College for the one-year senior service school course. These one-year tours happened precisely at the most disruptive time for him — right as he went through his sophomore and junior years. Justin went to public and Catholic schools, large and small, in four different parts of the country.

Through it all he excelled, despite the chaos caused by switching curricula and physical locations, not to mention his needing to make new friends each time we moved into a new community. To Justin's great credit, he made it all look easy, which it absolutely was not. No one would have blamed him if he felt sorry for himself or was angry towards us because of the constant change we made him go through. For this alone, I admire him, but there's so much more to him.

While starting his senior year at Tabb High School in Yorktown, Virginia, Justin began his search for which college to attend. Justin's grades were excellent, despite the crazy mix of courses he had to take to graduate. He also did well on his SAT tests, so he had a wide range of schools available to him. After visiting four or five colleges, Justin settled on James Madison University, a beautiful and prestigious school situated in the mountains of western Virginia. He enrolled in the very challenging Science and Technology program and, despite the intense rigor of the curriculum, he finished in the fall of 2001. This was just in time for the dot-com bust to be in full effect.

Unfortunately, this meant there were no technology jobs to be found anywhere, especially for a new college graduate. After searching for a technology-related job for six months, Justin took up an offer from his Uncle Paul (JoAnn's brother) to learn the electrical trade in Seattle, Washington, where Paul owned his own business as an electrical contractor. Justin moved to Seattle, became a licensed electrician and eventually started his own electrical contractor business (Queen Anne Electric), which he runs very successfully to this day.

In 2016, JoAnn and I had the chance to spend an entire summer near Justin and his family in Seattle and help some as his wife Jeanette recovered from extensive foot surgery. It was one of the highlights of my life. We hadn't, until that point, had the opportunity to live near him since he moved away to go to college in 1997. It was so joyous to see them and help and be involved with our two grandsons (Tom and Dane) without having to get on an airliner with all that entails. I deeply appreciate what both JoAnn and Justin brought into my life 30 years ago. I love them so very much and I would be far poorer in many ways without them.

Another example of JoAnn's and my trust in the Universe was a complete leap of faith. As I was finishing my tour in Belgium and concluding my military career in 2007, I ramped up my post-Air Force job search. As a colonel, I could only stay in the military for 30 years maximum, which is why I was retiring. The reason for my mandatory retirement is the "up-or-out" promotion system introduced by Congress in 1947 following World War II.

Before the war, the Army largely based promotion on seniority, whereby an officer would get promoted only when a more senior officer retired, separated, or died. The result was numerous older officers who held critical command and staff positions at the beginning of the war. Many of these senior officers weren't energetic enough or capable enough to perform their duties. Consequently, as the United States military services were trying to grow exponentially, they were also switching out many of their senior officers for younger ones deemed more capable — that's why a lieutenant colonel like Dwight Eisenhower could become a five-star general in just a few years.

The four services never wanted to go through that mess again. As our country transitioned into the Cold War, they created the up-or-out promotion system. Under this system, officers meet promotion boards at certain mandated times during their careers. If they get promoted, they get to continue with their military career. If they don't get promoted, and are instead "passed over," they must leave the military at a certain point. Since this topic is complicated, I go into more detail about specific officer ranks and the promotion system in Appendix B, if you're interested.

In a nutshell, an officer without any prior enlisted service must be promoted to major to be eligible for retirement benefits. A major must retire by 24 years, although most depart right after they hit 20. A lieutenant colonel must retire by 28 years and a colonel must retire by 30 years. In fact, the only officers who can go beyond 30 years are two-, three-, or four-star generals — a tiny fraction of 1 percent of the entire officer corps. Those of us who become career officers understand and accept this early on. There's nothing hidden or secret about the promotion system.

As I approached military retirement in the fall of 2006 and winter/spring of 2007, it was a very anxious time for a lot of reasons. At age 52, I was going on a job hunt for the first time since I joined the Air Force at age 18. My skills were very military-oriented. Apart from my extensive leadership experience, my job knowledge didn't translate readily to civilian positions. Perhaps most daunting, we were living in Belgium and I wanted to find a job in the United States. The only certainty in our lives was we had to leave Belgium and the Air Force by the end of August 2007. Apart from that, it was all open field running, which was scary unto itself.

Being a rather deliberate, focused person, I said "Okay, let's get to it" as the New Year started in January 2007. I took all the transition preparation courses the Air Force offered. I reached out to my defense industry contacts in Brussels to see if they could help spread my name/resume out amongst their colleagues. And I set up a 10-day job-hunting trip to San Diego for April of that year.

Like a normal couple, JoAnn and I wanted to live in a place we enjoyed (such as Germany, Monterey, and Belgium). Rather than spread out a nationwide net to find a job anywhere in the U.S., we focused on San Diego. We had gotten to know the area when we were stationed near Riverside. My uncle and aunt lived in San Diego and we loved it. I received pushback from many of my military and industry colleagues about the great difficulty we would undoubtedly encounter if we tried to find a position in San Diego.

They emphasized "that's a Navy and Marine town — there are no Air Force jobs there."

Still, we persevered. Before my job-hunting trip, I created a resume, did a lot of calling around, and set up four or five interviews with prospective employers — none of the interviews were for specific positions. JoAnn and Emily came along on our April trip as we also set aside time for house hunting. Two of the interviews resulted in some interest: one at SAIC in San Diego and another at Raytheon in El Segundo, two hours north of San Diego near Los Angeles. The SAIC interview was not planned — it resulted from a referral generated by one of the other companies I met with. They knew of an open SAIC position that might be a fit and they contacted SAIC on my behalf.

Meanwhile, JoAnn and I also found a house in San Diego we wanted to buy. It was in a great neighborhood right behind some good friends we were stationed with in Germany. Our daughters were very good friends, too, so it was a great match. It was perfect, except for two really big issues. The house cost three times as much as we had ever paid for a home before. And the housing market in early 2007 was starting to waver a bit even though prices were high. It would be a huge mess within a year, but we didn't know that then.

The second issue, of course, was that I didn't have a job — I had interest from two companies (one two hours away from the house we were looking at), but nothing firm at all. No offers. So, as we approached the end of our job- and house-hunting trip, we had to decide. Do we make an offer on the house or do we defer all of this until we show up in August after I'm out of the Air Force? We talked about it. We went through the pros and cons of each option. And then we decided to imagine the best possible outcome and take actions as if that's what would happen. We made an offer on the San Diego house and it was accepted. It was a complete act of trust in the Universe. It was faith that all will turn out well if we trust it will.

We returned to Belgium at the end of our 10-day trip and I went back to work. As time went on and the two positions I interviewed for failed to materialize, JoAnn and I began to second-guess ourselves. Did we actually buy an expensive house when I didn't even have a job yet? What the hell were we thinking? We were out driving around Brussels one afternoon, talking about this situation and getting increasingly more anxious. We decided to stop, be thankful about what amazing creators we are, and ask for an indication everything would be okay. JoAnn had recently heard feathers were a sign of angels being present. That sounded good to me. So, we asked to see feathers to let us know we were on the right path.

As we returned home that day, we turned the corner on the street to our house and there it was on our front lawn. A huge pile of white feathers. At first, there were so many feathers we were concerned the man who mowed our lawn might have made an unscheduled visit and run over some birds with the lawn mower. We got out of our car and walked over to the pile. Slowly, I sifted through the feathers to see if there were any bird bodies in there. There weren't. It was exactly what it looked like: a giant pile of feathers on our front lawn. We had no idea where they came from and we never found out. We also didn't question the meaning of this sign. Everything was going to be okay. We just needed to trust.

As spring turned into summer, the anxiety was still present, but to a lesser degree. Both JoAnn and I saw feathers on a regular basis. On one occasion, I even saw some in a hallway, inside the embassy. As we came closer to our July 26th departure from Belgium, I continued to follow up with my contacts at SAIC and Raytheon to remind them of my interest and to ask if there was anything I could do to assist. In June, Raytheon gave me a call to let me know the position they had targeted for me had just gone away. Don't worry, they said, they really wanted to hire me. They only needed to find another suitable position. Well, that wasn't encouraging.

Then, on July 1, less than four weeks before I departed for the U.S., I came home after running a Belgian marathon between the cities of Kortrijk and Bruges (with all its beautiful canals). I checked my email and there it was. A job offer from SAIC. They wanted me to start two weeks after I got to San Diego. I felt as if an enormous weight had been lifted from my shoulders. The two-week gap would even allow us to receive our shipments of household goods before I started work. JoAnn and I breathed a sigh of relief and thanked God and our angels for our blessings. Again.

Chapter 29

Joyful Landings

Emily, JoAnn, and me in Maui in 2016.

As my T-38 sped through the West Texas night at 180 MPH, I made my decision. I swallowed hard and asked for permission to again try a visual overhead pattern to a touch-and-go landing. This was the exact maneuver that almost killed me only seconds before. A touch-and-go is where a plane lands on the runway and, instead of stopping the aircraft, the pilot pushes up the power to take off again without slowing down. The controller gave me approval to proceed. I calmed down and set myself up to try it again. My heart was still pounding, and I was more than a little afraid. Gone was the complete confidence I had before.

I turned towards downwind and began to fly a much wider pattern than I needed, resulting in a very controlled box pattern to a touch-and-go landing. I was taking no chances. After I lifted off from the runway, I then requested another overhead pattern to a touch-and-go. This next time, I made adjustments and my second pattern and landing was tighter and more like what I had done in the past. I then asked for one last overhead pattern to a full-stop landing since I was at minimum fuel due to my extensive afterburner use. My final pattern and landing were perfect. I allowed myself to smile. As I taxied back into parking, I felt relieved and more than a little proud of myself for facing my fears . . .

As the fertility doctor at the Reproductive Resource Center prescribed, over the course of the next few weeks JoAnn took multiple medications, including daily hormone shots I administered to increase her egg count. At the same time, she had to give up smoking completely. She smoked only occasionally, but it was still a part of her life. It was one of the most difficult times of her life to give up smoking and be pumped full of extra hormones, and I admire her greatly for it and am thankful to this day.

When the time came, after all the shots had taken effect, JoAnn had her eggs harvested by the RRC medical staff. They removed three healthy ones. Meanwhile, I was busy "donating" my sperm in the special lounge in the RRC built for that purpose, complete with appropriate picture magazines. For some time afterwards, the running joke in our family was "at least one of us had fun that day."

The RRC staff then carefully prepared JoAnn's eggs by removing some of the outer protective layer — they did this to make it easier for my sperm to penetrate her eggs. My sperm were placed in the same dish as her eggs, with the hope at least one pair would successfully find each other. We went home that night and prayed. We didn't just pray God would do what was best for all of us. More than that, we declared that we knew whatever happened, we understood it was for the best and we were very grateful.

The next day, we were very excited to learn, against the odds, that one egg had fertilized. We went back to the clinic to have the egg implanted into JoAnn's womb. Before this happened, we looked at the fertilized egg through a microscope. This was thrilling to see our beautiful two-celled embryo — we even named it Ernie the Embryo. We had a chance. We had a real chance to have a baby of our own. It was November 3rd, a day we would mark on our calendar. More on this miracle later.

The most recent example of our needing to trust and have faith came just a few years ago. By the spring of 2015, my company had promoted me to a position in charge of the San Diego operations of our cybersecurity division. While I appreciated the promotion, the great pay, and my excellent bosses, I found I was working close to 12-hour days and routinely putting in time on weekends. Even then, I would wake up in the middle of the night and think about things I needed to remember for the next day. I was burning the candle at both ends and nothing on the horizon looked to change. JoAnn jokingly suggested I might want to consider leaving the job at Leidos (by this time, SAIC had split into two and the part I went with was renamed Leidos). I didn't want to. We had a home with a mortgage and I couldn't see how we could manage to have enough money to live a comfortable lifestyle without me working for at least five or six more years. That is, if I could continue to dodge getting laid off, which had been a continuous threat to all of us in leadership positions ever since the recession.

Many of the managers I worked with when I joined the company in 2007 were gone, forced into retirement when the 2008 recession hit, and government contracts became far scarcer. The reason I was working such long days was because there was still work to do, but the company had reduced the number of managers available to do it. In other words, when new work came around, rather than hire a new manager, the company just added that job onto the work for an existing manager. Expenses went down, but the work day got longer. And I felt fortunate. At least I had a job.

Then came tax season in the spring of 2015. Because we had remodeled part of our house in Encinitas, we needed to dip into my IRA. I was over 59 ½, so I didn't have to pay a penalty. What I had to do was declare that money as income. The result was that when my income from Leidos was added to my military pension combined with my IRA withdrawal, we were subject to the Alternative Minimum Tax (AMT) for the first time. The AMT, created in 1982, was designed to ensure high earners paid a minimum amount of taxes each year by subjecting them to a different set of tax calculations when income was above a certain level. It was brutal. Instead of getting a large refund as I anticipated, we owed $8,000.

Now, "making too much money" sounds like a good problem to have. I'm not going to complain about that. What this did was cause me to question why am I working so hard if I'm going to pay so much of my income back to the government in income taxes? JoAnn and I looked hard at what we had coming in. We looked at our expenses, too. We also knew Emily was finishing her teaching credential in a month and the Dublin School District had already hired her to teach freshman biology. This meant we wouldn't be paying her college expenses any more. We had just paid off both of our cars, as well. As we looked at the situation, we saw the only recurring major expense we had was our rather large house payment.

How important was it to hold on to our house? This was a question we had never asked before. After moving so many times in the Air Force, where we had only occasionally owned a home throughout the years, it was almost an article of faith we needed to own a home now that we weren't subject to a military-ordered move on short notice. And even when we had owned a home, it was only those times we expected to be in a location for at least three years — which worked out just once. We were fortunate to break even each of those times when we sold.

We looked at the numbers. I went through them multiple times. I looked at what our current home was worth on the market. We sat down and talked. "I think we can do it," I said. "We can sell the house. I can leave my job. We have enough coming in between my pension and what we've saved to cover our expenses. That is, if we downsize, now it's just the two of us."

We looked at each other. I felt both fear and excitement. This was a major step into the unknown. Could we do it? Where would we go? How would I adjust to not having a full-time career for the first time in my life? We asked each other how we felt about this. JoAnn told me if I wanted to take this step, she was all for it. We trusted the Universe to take care of us. We would put our house up for sale.

Two weeks after making that decision, I had a business trip to Washington, DC, to meet with my boss and other company leadership to go over a major proposal for a $1 billion multiple-award Air Force contract. Being the lead for this proposal was one of my many roles. During that trip, my boss (Karen Anderson, who is a superb leader) told me she was reorganizing her division. She wanted to consolidate her San Diego activities and wanted me to continue to lead them — the organization would be more streamlined, and the lines of authority would be clearer.

Having a lot of responsibility without having authority over the people I led was part of the problem I faced. Our organization chart was convoluted, and I was responsible for quite a few people I had no authority over. I told Karen I was honored by her confidence in me, but I had decided to stop working full time for Leidos. She wasn't surprised. I think she had sensed my frustration even though she was very happy with my performance and we got along well. I offered to stay on in a part-time, as-needed consulting capacity. The large Air Force proposal I was leading was very important for our people in San Diego and the company as a whole. I wanted to see it through to a successful conclusion. She agreed.

Telling Karen about my decision was an act of faith. I didn't want to leave the job immediately. JoAnn and I needed to sell our house, which takes months of preparation, marketing, and closing. We also wanted to move out of our house, putting most of our belongings in permanent storage. We decided we would just keep several suitcases worth of belongings, so we could travel easily. Anything we wanted to keep out that we couldn't take with us on an airliner would go into a temporary storage unit in San Diego. JoAnn and I had even decided where we wanted to go.

We had always loved Hawaii, and we wanted to spend time on Maui. Just the two of us, with our cat Pierre. Little did he know what an adventure was in store for him. Altogether, I wanted a good four or five months to get ready for all of this. By telling Karen as early as I did, I was taking the risk the company would put me on two weeks' notice once they found out I was intending to leave. I was trusting Karen to work with me on my transition out and someone else's transition into my role(s).

Fortunately, Karen and I were of the same mind. She didn't want me to leave any sooner than I had planned. This would allow her to find someone to take my position. It would, if the schedule held out, also give us enough time to produce and submit our huge Air Force proposal. In the meantime, she appreciated me letting her know. It would give her time to make any adjustments she needed to. For the time being, though, we would just keep it between us.

The next five months went quickly, even though there was a huge amount of activity. We sold our house and sorted all our stuff into stay, go, or give-away categories. We ended up donating a lot of what we owned. We didn't need it and we didn't want to pay to store it. My remaining time at Leidos was successful even though the Air Force pushed back the proposal into the Spring of 2016. This was a good thing for me, as I could stay on with the company and work from home as we put together the proposal, which we won. I've remained with Leidos in a "remote" capacity, working from my home on different Department of Defense proposals as the company needs me.

JoAnn and Pierre and I went to Maui in October 2015 and thoroughly enjoyed island life through the end of May 2016. After spending six fun months in Hawaii, we missed our children and grandchildren, being multiple time zones and an ocean away from them. We returned to the West Coast in June 2016, although we didn't go right back to San Diego. We spent the summer of 2016 in Seattle living near Justin, Jeanette, and our two grandsons — one of the most wonderful times in my life.

Justin and Jeanette were married in 2007 and Tom and Dane were born in 2009 and 2011. We had never lived near them. Every time we wanted to get together, we had to fly up there, or they came down to San Diego, or we would meet someplace else. By living in Seattle for almost three months, we could have a normalized, more routine relationship with them. It was great — one of the best summers I ever remember.

We returned to San Diego in the fall of 2016, where we remain. We live in a small, rented house in a nice, quiet neighborhood. Life is a lot more relaxed. I've even found time to start a writing career with this book — something I've wanted to do for many years. I'm so very grateful we trusted our guidance and decided to change our lifestyle in 2015.

The woman hired to take my place as the San Diego leader did a great job, but the position went away one year later due to downsizing and restructuring. I'm certain if I had tried to continue with the company, the company would have downsized me, too. I now work occasionally at Leidos as a company consultant. Because I left my full-time position in an organized manner, I could take the time to coordinate my departure and leave on my own terms. Without the trust we had in our angels and in each other, JoAnn and I would have missed this golden opportunity. Our mindset of trusting started that evening so many years ago as JoAnn and I prayed for a child and left it in the hands of God . . .

Chapter 30

New Chapter

My mother's engagement photo in 1941.

"Your mother stopped drinking."

My father was on the other end of the phone. He had called me at my apartment in Louisiana.

"Wait. Are you sure? This doesn't make sense."

He reassured me that's what happened. He hadn't wanted to talk about it until he was certain she quit. After a couple of months, he decided it was time to let the rest of the family know.

My mother stopped drinking after her treatment at rehab during Christmas, 1986. There was a relapse shortly afterward, but then, she just stopped. Not another drink. This wasn't clear to us for a while. I'm not sure it was clear to anybody right then.

I was stunned. I was excited it might be true, but I didn't want my hopes to get raised. There had been way too many disappointments before. After more time went along, it became apparent she had, in fact, stopped drinking. Our prayers had been answered. But questions welled up within me. Why did this happen now? What caused it to work this time? Most of all, though, if Mom could just "stop drinking" on her own, why in the hell didn't she do it years ago?

Over the years since, Mom's stated reason for getting sober was, "Your father stopped trying to control me." Her wanting to blame him for her drinking showed she didn't want to take responsibility for her actions. She never wanted to talk about her drinking. Until the end of her life, she half-apologized for all the pain, chaos, and embarrassment she caused. She didn't want to go deep into it. I'm guessing it was because it would be too painful for her to admit the trauma she had caused.

I'm very grateful that by the time I met JoAnn in the summer of 1988, my mother's drinking was behind her. Once Mom became sober in 1987, she was wonderful to be around. When my daughter Emily came along in 1991, she and Mom became best friends until my Mom passed on in 2002. I love that JoAnn, Justin, and Emily have no memories of my mother and alcohol. They remember her as a loving, if somewhat eccentric, mother-in-law and grandmother, devoted to all of us and the rest of her family. I'm happy it's this way, because that's a true reflection of her real self.

What have I learned from my mother's alcoholism? The most valuable thing is how very important it is to be reliable, consistent, and considerate, especially with those I love. I hope I have expressed that to my family, most importantly, but also to friends and colleagues I interact with every day. I appreciate this lesson and I also know my Mom's alcoholism, to a large degree, helped inspire me to move far away from home and join the Air Force.

The Air Force also meant adventure. I was far more drawn to the Air Force for the excitement and challenge it offered than any need I had to run away from home. Still, I remember that day in January 1978, when, a month after my 23rd birthday, I got in my Toyota Corolla and drove away from Los Altos — the place where I had lived my entire life. I had lots of great friends and many good memories.

The decision to join the Air Force was a springboard to many of the successes I had in my life. Of course, my father's heroic example influenced me heavily. I also wanted to just get the hell away from all the craziness and chaos. I wanted to go someplace where I could count on people and where they behaved consistently. I wanted schedules and structure and a system of rewards if I performed well. That meant the Air Force.

While in pilot training, I never got homesick, wishing I could be "back home" and away from the constant stress in that environment. This was different from many of my classmates. Once I left home and began my life in the Air Force, I committed to making it a success. I wasn't going back.

I also want to highlight some of the many good things Mom taught me — lessons I could appreciate even more after she stopped drinking. She was as kind and generous as anyone I've ever met. She wanted to give love and be loved by those around her. As time has passed since my Mom's death, I can appreciate her many loving qualities even more, while I understand how her alcoholic behavior helped teach me the importance of being trustworthy and learning to trust again.

Chapter 31

Emily

Our beautiful daughter Emily in 2010 (Age 19).

JoAnn stood at the top of the stairs as I came through the front door. She had tears in her eyes and a smile on her face. I held my breath.

"I'm pregnant."

I started crying, too, as we hugged each other closely. Justin was also very excited. I was going to have a child of my own and Justin would have a little brother or sister. Our miracle baby was on its way.

A week earlier, we were overjoyed when we received the news one of JoAnn's eggs had fertilized. We even saw the dividing embryo under a microscope. The next huge step was for the egg to attach itself to JoAnn's uterus. After the doctor implanted her fertilized egg, we had to wait for days to find out if it had attached and JoAnn was pregnant. It seemed like forever, but at least now there was a chance. After all this time, I was afraid to get my hopes up that the "impossible" might become a reality — that JoAnn might be pregnant, and we would have a baby.

I remember it was a Friday in November 1990 when the clinic told us they would know the results. I would be studying at Command and General Staff College that day, as usual. On my drive from school, knowing JoAnn would have already received the phone call at home, I stopped by a florist and bought a dozen roses for her. I wanted her to know, whatever the outcome, I loved and cherished her dearly. When I walked up to our front door, I saw a child's flightsuit hanging on the doorknob. JoAnn had placed it there. I wanted to believe it meant what I thought it might. I opened the door, roses in hand, and went in the house.

After we received the miraculous news JoAnn was pregnant, we went through a healthy pregnancy, including the discovery that our baby was a girl. On July 30, 1991, our beautiful daughter Emily was born. In addition to her birthday, each year we also fondly remember November 3rd as "Ernie the Embryo Day". We do that to remind us of one of the happiest days of our lives — the day we discovered, against the odds, one of JoAnn's eggs had fertilized.

Emily was a delight from the beginning. She shares many of her mother's traits — they both are beautiful, intelligent, and have very big hearts. Emily also has her mother's delightfully ironic sense of humor. The room lights up when she enters.

Emily has an amazing ability to make new friends and stay close to old friends she has made throughout the years. She has a large cadre of wonderful, close friends from grade school, high school, and college. She adores them, and they adore her. Far from seeing all our moves in the Air Force as a hardship, she embraced each new duty station as an opportunity for adventure, exploration, and making new friends.

Emily has blossomed into a wonderful, accomplished young woman. Her college years were particularly impressive, as she made such a positive impact on her professors that they encouraged her to run for the student senate at Sonoma State University at the end of her freshman year. She did, was elected, and she ran for a second term the next year and was reelected.

She developed such poise the faculty recommended she become a paid peer mentor for incoming freshman students. This experience inspired her to go into teaching as a full-time profession.

Emily is enjoying her life as a biology teacher at Dublin High School in the San Francisco Bay Area. She was married in July of 2018 in a beautiful ceremony in the redwoods outside of Santa Cruz. Her husband Chris is a very nice young man Emily met at Sonoma State where they earned their degrees in marine biology. I could not possibly be prouder.

So, what did I learn from the sometimes difficult, but ultimately joyous series of events surrounding our pregnancy experience? Apart from a deep appreciation for JoAnn, Justin, and Emily, I learned a man's value is not measured by his ability to procreate. When faced with the near certainty I would never father a child, I had to take a deep look at what being a man was all about and those qualities that defined me as a man.

I knew, after all I wanted and all was said and done, that I would not let my sperm count define me. The contributions I could make in life are not solely focused on raising children. As hard as it was to take, this was a vital understanding for me to have. My accomplishments and the people I impact go far beyond my family, despite the centrality of my wife, children, and grandchildren to my life. I am grateful for this understanding.

I also learned to love and appreciate my children on a deep level. JoAnn's love and support throughout this ordeal was beyond amazing. I wouldn't have dealt with this experience nearly as well without her care and understanding. And because well-meaning medical experts told me I would never have children of my own, this may have only increased my appreciation of my children more than if Emily's arrival had been easier or less problematic. For that, I am grateful, for Emily and Justin have enriched my life beyond measure.

The most important lesson I've learned is the need for trust. I had to trust my beloved partner even though this was hard to do because of what happened with my previous marriage. My faith has only expanded since we married in 1989. While it has taken time, I believe my journey on this path began in earnest the night JoAnn's one fertilized egg was implanted in her. We expressed our gratitude and our knowing that whatever will be is coming about because of the infinite love and power of the divine presence in this world. It is such a comfort to have that belief.

While I'm nowhere near being finished, I'm very satisfied with where I am right now. I feel great about what I've done with my life and the positive impact I feel I've made on those around me. Not everything I've touched has turned to gold — far from it. But I believe I've approached each situation and each person in my life with courage, compassion, integrity, and trust. Because of this, I have no lingering regrets. I don't dwell on failures I've had because I know I've done my best. This feeling of satisfaction is worth more than I can describe. And I owe much of my success to the lessons I've learned.

The array of experiences I described here have all helped shape me into the man I've become. Even though many of these events were difficult and often very painful, they have also been the greatest teaching experiences of my life. Without them, I wouldn't be the man I am now. I hope to continue to be inspired by them for the rest of my life.

PART 5

REINVENTION

Me speaking on stage in Las Vegas in 2018.
(Christina Nefaris)

Chapter 32

Our Need for Reinvention

*Major General Nick Williams, 21st Air Force commander,
presenting me with the Legion of Merit award at the conclusion of my
two-year tour in command of the 19th Air Refueling Group. The next day
I flew to Germany to begin a six-year stretch of three different assignments
focused on supporting U.S. military operations in Europe. Every one of those
assignments required me to reinvent myself. On the right is Colonel Barb
Faulkenberry, my replacement in the 19th. While I was not involved in this
decision, I could not have picked a better officer to take over for me.
(U.S. Air Force)*

As I described earlier, I survived pilot training, my mother's alcoholism,
my abusive sixth-grade teacher, my divorce, and my struggles with infertility.
All of us know, though, that life is much more than merely surviving. I
believe we are meant to thrive. We are meant to enjoy life. Just like that
night at pilot training in 1978, though, our lives can change in a heartbeat.

Jobs go away, and different opportunities arise. Relationships end, and new ones begin. We live in an environment where change is a constant.

This frequent change requires us to reinvent ourselves. That night in Texas, the runway I needed to land on changed. There was an unexpected wind shear, and when I found myself in a very dangerous situation, I couldn't continue flying my approach as I had planned. It was obvious I needed to make instant, dramatic changes. Even in the immediacy of that moment, though, I still needed to create a new plan, trust in my abilities, and have the discipline and skill to carry it out. And I needed to do all of it very quickly.

Life has clearly shown me you don't have to change jobs to need to reinvent yourself. For 30 years, I had the same employer: The United States Air Force. Yet, during my career as an officer, the Air Force assigned me to numerous positions requiring radically different skills and knowledge from anything I had ever done before. While I started off as a pilot, throughout my career the Air Force wanted me to do a wide variety of high-visibility jobs that had nothing to do with flying.

I had 16 different assignments while I was on active duty. Besides packing up and moving each time, my new assignments required me to reinvent myself, as I needed to master new skills, learn a new body of knowledge, and refocus my efforts. My biggest reinvention, however, was when I reached my 30-year maximum service limit in the Air Force. At age 52 and with a daughter getting ready to go to college, I had to completely reinvent myself as a software development program manager, a job I had to learn from scratch.

My story is not unique by any means. Every one of us goes through change. That often means we need to reinvent ourselves. Most jobs we do today weren't even dreamed of when I graduated from college in 1977. And if the job is still with us, it's being done in a radically different way. All of us need to update our skills and learn something unexpected and new to continue moving forward and thriving. This means reinventing ourselves.

There are different ways to approach change. We can view it with fear and indecision where we see ourselves as victims without any control of the decisions and direction in our lives; but approaching change from this perspective would be akin to letting go of my aircraft controls and trusting everything will work out perfectly. And while it's very important to have faith and trust in the goodness of the Universe, there are times when we need to take decisive action. That night in Texas, I could not let things unfold any further and see what would happen. I needed to act. If we are in a situation where we feel inspired to reinvent ourselves, the best way to approach it is with an attitude of positive action and the intent to take control of our lives.

Sometimes, like that night in Texas, an immediate decision is required. If that's the case, follow your instincts, decide what to do, and take action. Don't look back. Almost always, though, there is time to gather data and make an informed decision. This does not mean procrastination; although there are times when you might be faced with bad alternatives and the best course of action is to wait a bit longer to see if something better develops. If that's where you find yourself, it may be wiser to make a conscious choice to delay your decision.

Apart from these situations, the best alternative is almost always to take positive action. The best way to do this is often from a deliberate, holistic perspective. What's important in your life? Have you reconnected with your values and principles? Where do you find inspiration? Do you need to rekindle your inspiration? Answering these questions can help you retake control of your life in a situation where you might feel powerless. They can help you find your own personal aim point. I'll talk more about my "AIM POINT" in the next chapters. Taking control also allows you the freedom to feel inspired by your choices rather than feeling as if you've been pushed into something you don't want.

Look at the changes you are facing right now. I know they can feel overwhelming. At the end of my career, the Air Force assigned me to a position completely different from anything I had ever done. I became the Chief of the Office of Defense Cooperation at the American Embassy in Brussels. My team of officers and I worked directly for the U.S. Ambassador to Belgium. I had little knowledge regarding what the roles and responsibilities of the position entailed, yet there I was: the guy in charge. Not only that, the Air Force had sent my wife and me to French-language school so we could at least attempt to talk with the Belgian military and government representatives in their own language. And, of course, our family had to move from the United States to Europe; this even included our two family cats. As exciting as all of this was, it was also overwhelming.

And then one of my life's most embarrassing events occurred. During my first week on the job, I was meeting with a Belgian defense contractor in downtown Brussels (the capital of Belgium). I remember having difficulty even finding the restaurant, not to mention a parking space, among the narrow, winding backstreets of the city, so I was a little late. While the contractor and I were talking and eating lunch, a piece of meat got stuck in my throat, clogging my windpipe. It soon became clear I was choking. The gentleman I was meeting with got up and slapped me on the back. That was enough to do the trick. It helped dislodge the piece of meat and I started breathing normally.

While I didn't die physically, I did nearly die of embarrassment. It was a terrible start to what turned out to be a fantastic assignment. And there's no question in my mind that my choking at the restaurant was directly related to me feeling choked and overwhelmed by the responsibilities and requirements of this new position I held.

This story has a happy ending. I learned the responsibilities of my new job without further medical incident. After about one year in my position, both the U.S. and Belgium asked me to preside over a bilateral conference between our two air forces. The issue at hand was the Belgian desire to purchase American-made targeting pods for their F-16 fighters. This was important to the U.S. military far beyond the small size of the Belgian purchase.

Since Belgium was our country's first North Atlantic Treaty Organization (NATO) ally who was purchasing the American-made targeting pod (instead of the European version), it would help the U.S. defense industry to make inroads into this market. More importantly, it would make Belgium's air force more compatible with the U.S. Air Force since we would all be using the same equipment. It would also set the stage for our other, larger European allies to buy the American pods. Everyone wanted this to happen.

The problem was, since this was the first time Lockheed Martin was going to sell their targeting pods to someone outside the United States, the U.S. Air Force contracting community attached expensive setup costs to this contract, per their regulations. These additional fees increased the overall program cost from $21 million to $31 million. Because of political forces and financial constraints within Belgium, if the price couldn't come down to $21 million, the Belgians would have to purchase the significantly cheaper European targeting pods. In a last-ditch attempt to come to an agreement, we all gathered at Robins Air Force Base in the United States for a three-day negotiation to see what might be done. I sensed there was little optimism on either side going into the negotiation.

Fortunately, though, I was the senior officer present and was able to set the proper tone right off the bat. I began our conference by reminding everyone of our common goal: to come to a mutual agreement on this contract all parties would embrace. I assured them my goal was to ensure everyone present had a chance to voice their opinions and concerns. I also emphasized there would be no pressure on anyone to accept a position they were uncomfortable with.

The relief in the room was palpable. After three days, the Belgians had pulled back some of their requirements, reducing the overall costs somewhat. American acquisition representatives adjusted their perspectives on what they considered Belgium's fair share of the setup costs — this reduced the costs tremendously.

By the time we finished, we negotiated the price down to $21 million and everyone left happy. The senior Belgian officer present approached me afterwards to tell me he was in disbelief we had come to an agreement — he didn't think it was possible before the meeting. Four months later, a similar situation arose on a different contract regarding purchase of modern helmet-mounted displays for the Belgian F-16s. The first thing the Belgians and the Americans did was arrange for a negotiating conference. Both sides asked for me specifically to preside over the gathering. I went from choking to chairman in a little more than a year. Not bad.

But that's often how it goes when you reinvent yourself. You start by being the new person and not even knowing where you're even supposed to sit in the office, much less wondering what you're supposed to be doing at that moment. You wonder why you even made this change. You may want to quit. All these thoughts have gone through my head when I've had to reinvent myself.

Before long, though, people are coming to you for advice. After that, they see you as the expert. Then you become the visionary. The next thing you know, you're giving the keynote address at the annual convention. You may think I'm exaggerating, but I'm not. This can happen to you. The first step is accepting that you sometimes need to reinvent yourself. The best place to start your reinvention process is by defining your own core guidelines and principles. This is what AIM POINT is all about.

Chapter 33

Finding Our Aim Point

Speaking to a gathering before I retired from the Air Force.
The move from career military officer to software program manager
was the biggest reinvention challenge of my life. So far.

Just like when I was flying in the Air Force, every one of us needs a guidance system to go where we want to go. Once I finished the first four parts of this book describing the events and people surrounding my life, I thought about my guidance system. I wanted to share my insights with you.

I've summarized my guideposts into an easy to remember eight-letter acronym: AIM POINT. When a pilot lines up on final approach, he or she needs to pick an aim point in the runway's touchdown zone to make a safe landing. Just like that pilot, we all need to have aim points throughout our lives. Here are my aim points, my guideposts — I will write about them each in a little more detail in the following chapters:

207

A = Appreciation

I = Integrity

M = Make a Decision

P = Prioritize Play

O = Set Objectives and Goals

I = Inspiration

N = Nurture

T = Trust

My life has been amazing, exhilarating, satisfying, and joyful. My life has also been frightening and humbling, and I've made many decisions that were far from perfect. Yet I believe I've approached each set of circumstances intending to do the best I could and for that, I feel grateful.

As you continue to read, I invite you to look at the circumstances of your life. Look at the people in your life. Do you appreciate them as much as you can, even when they're difficult? Do you approach your life and the decisions you make with integrity? Are you making decisions, making yourself known — do you offer your thoughts and opinions to others? Do you make play a priority, so your energy is renewed for other areas in your life? Do you have objectives and goals and are you happy with them? Do you seek out inspiration in your work and in your personal life? Do you nurture others and allow others to nurture you? Do you trust others; do you trust in a higher spirit?

There are no wrong answers to any of these questions. I offer them only as a way to do a self-inventory regarding where you are and compare it to where you want to be. The great news is that by becoming aware of these guidelines, you can help chart your own personal aim points and achieve your goals in life. Just as important, you can help create more joy in your life by creating an environment more consistent with what you want. This is the first step in reinventing yourself — determining what's important in your life, what inspires you, and reconnecting with your core values and principles. The next eight chapters in this book introduce each of the AIM POINT guidelines, so you can have a clearer idea of my perspective.

Chapter 34

Appreciation

*Grandson Tom, daughter-in-law Jeanette, Emily,
new son-in-law Chris, JoAnn, Justin, and grandson Dane at
Emily's and Chris's wedding in 2018. Joyful appreciation for
each of them is one of the cornerstones of my life.*

"Appreciation is a wonderful thing. It makes what is excellent in others belong to us as well."

*Voltaire, French Enlightenment writer,
historian and philosopher*

The first, and perhaps most important, AIM POINT guideline is Appreciation. Our appreciation for those around us and for our present situation defines who we are by our outlook on life. By having an attitude of appreciation, we also attract more of the same into our lives. Appreciation given to others generates appreciation coming our way from them. While it's easy to appreciate people and things when life is going well, it's even more important to focus on appreciation when we hit bumps in our lives. Making it more personal, if someone in your family is being difficult, focus on what you appreciate about them. If you don't care for your job, focus on some specific things or people you like at work.

Another way to look at this is you get more of what you focus on. If you appreciate your friends, loved ones, and other people in your life, they will appreciate you even more. I've made a point to do my best to treat all people whom I deal with, whether in a personal or professional capacity, with respect, compassion, and appreciation. Besides getting a friendly response, which is enough reward in itself, I've also found showing appreciation is great for selfish reasons. Apart from strengthening my relationships, that salesclerk or the airline ticket representative or my server at a restaurant will bend over backward to help me if I treat them with dignity and show appreciation for what they're doing for me. Approaching everyone with a positive, appreciative attitude as a matter of habit is the best way to go.

Conversely, on those occasions when I've been frustrated or in a bad mood, I can sense people digging in their heels and coming up with reasons why they can't do what I want. That's when I have to stop myself, take a step back, and recalibrate my attitude. Sometimes, I even need to simply step away from the situation and try again later. Escalating my anger and trying to "brute-force" a solution usually results in hard feelings and an imperfect solution, even though I might "win" the fight.

We all live in the real world, and I will be the first to say that sometimes it's necessary to make our point clearly and candidly to get what we want. Being a doormat doesn't help. Yet, we need to be very, very careful before deciding to thump our chests and declare ourselves as the alpha male/female, because we can easily strain or damage relationships. We may want that same person to cooperate with us somewhere down the road. Good luck with that if we've already applied a scorched-earth policy with them.

If you sense I advocate adopting something of a "Pollyanna" attitude, you're exactly right. Pollyanna was a cheerful and optimistic orphan girl in a children's book written more than 100 years ago. For someone to be known as a "Pollyanna" implies they aren't looking at a situation realistically. I would argue that's how we should be, as a matter of habit. We can be aware of our situation with all its problems and warts, yet consciously choose to focus on appreciation as a matter of routine. All of us will be much better off if we make appreciation and optimism our default position.

Chapter 35

Integrity

*"Integrity First" is the #1 core value of the U.S. Air Force.
(camouflagepatterns.wordpress.com)*

"If you don't have integrity, you have nothing. You can't buy it. You can have all the money in the world, but if you are not a moral and ethical person, you really have nothing."

*Henry Kravis, American businessman,
investor, and philanthropist.*

I've talked about integrity earlier, so I'll only touch base on it here. Integrity is one of the four areas I wrote about at length as part of this book, so clearly, I believe it's important.

The main point I'd like to make is this: Be truthful. Be honest. It is in our best interests to live this way. If we make our decisions and conduct our lives from a moral and ethical perspective, we won't find ourselves wondering what we told this or that person the last time we talked with them. More importantly, we won't feel the need to hide our motivations or our past decisions. Living a life of integrity frees us from these self-imposed chains and helps us sleep more peacefully.

In addition to freeing us from self-doubt and fear, others will respect us for having integrity. They will give us the benefit of the doubt. They will trust us to do the right thing, even when they're not around. They will be more willing to negotiate with us to come up with a mutually agreeable solution to a problem. The support we receive from others is priceless. Having a reputation for integrity is indispensable to success in our work and personal lives. Whatever immediate gain we might receive from using a deceitful shortcut pales compared to the damage we do to our reputation and the loss of self-esteem that comes from dishonesty.

It's important to be forthright, as well. We can still be compassionate and polite while being honest and direct — these aren't mutually exclusive. Having integrity doesn't mean being inflexible. We all need to cooperate with others. Being honest and considerate regarding everyone's thoughts and desires will lead others to react the same way, which then helps create the best outcome for everyone. Having a "my way or the highway" attitude rarely helps.

Finally, don't expect yourself or others to be perfect. All of us, me included, have fallen short regarding integrity on occasion — usually this comes from fear of confrontation or fear of a negative outcome. When we find ourselves in a situation where we haven't acted with complete integrity, the best thing we can do is admit our mistake and do what we can to make the situation better. Most people are forgiving, and they will respect us for being forthcoming. It's also important to be kind to yourself. Recognize you're doing your best. Take what has happened as a learning experience and move on from there.

Chapter 36

Make a Decision

(rypeapp.com)

"The most difficult thing is the decision to act, the rest is merely tenacity. The fears are paper tigers. You can do anything you decide to do. You can act to change and control your life; and the procedure, the process, is its own reward."

Amelia Earhart, American aviation pioneer

When we face our fears, two things happen. We make ourselves known and we make a decision. These have both been crucial to my happiness and success in life. So, let's start with make yourself known. Many of us live under the mistaken belief if we stay quiet and don't offer our opinions, people will like us more. Nothing could be further from the truth. This is something I need to watch, too. People want our inputs. We have so many valuable things to offer. By staying silent, we rob the group of our insight and wisdom.

The fear associated with not speaking up is rooted in the fear of being seen as ignorant or not worthy, which can lead to rejection. In healthy, mature groups, this fear is unfounded, as all members recognize encouraging everyone to offer their thoughts is essential to achieving the group's goals. Still, I fully understand that group dynamics can be uncomfortable; I often reserve my opinion until some other members have offered their inputs. This is particularly true if I'm not an expert on the topic being discussed or if I'm in a leadership position.

You may have found once "the boss" gives his or her opinion, others in the group will often line up to support their leader. It's human nature. Because of that, when leading a discussion, I find it's best to ask for others' inputs at the beginning of the meeting. I want to be sure they have a chance to provide their expertise and opinions before I offer mine. With some team members, it may be necessary to solicit their inputs privately due to their reluctance to speak up. You may have also found some of the best inputs come from the quietest and most reserved members of the team — that certainly has been my experience.

When not in a leadership position, I suggest giving inputs before the boss begins to steer the conversation. I find if I wait too long, the opportunity to influence any decisions may have waned. Of course, there are times when we may feel our level of knowledge on the subject may not be as deep as we'd like. On those occasions, we may want to wait until we have a more well-formed question or input before we speak up. It's okay to be quiet while you form an opinion or gather your thoughts. Everyone will value your input even more. Don't quiet your own voice because you're worried about how others will react. Your silence is not good for the group and it's especially not good for you and your self-esteem.

What I described above centers on a professional setting. The same principles apply even more so to our friends and loved ones. Offering our opinion is critical for our relationships. Those people who are important to us want us to express ourselves, not just go along with the program. Let them know what you want. If, for whatever reason, they routinely resist your inputs, you may want to reexamine your relationship with them.

"Every time you make the hard, correct decision you become a bit more courageous, and every time you make the easy, wrong decision you become a bit more cowardly."

Ben Horowitz, American businessman,
investor, blogger, and author

Now let's look at the need to make a decision. The need for decision-making is crucial to success. Many times, when facing a difficult decision, we often let it slide until it becomes "overcome by events." There are times when we must choose between painful alternatives where the best course is not to decide until we either have more information or a better alternative presents itself. The "decision to wait" should be a conscious choice, though, rather than the lack of a decision.

By refusing to make a decision in our lives, we give our power away to other people or future events. The result will be, by definition, something we didn't choose. It may not be something we want at all. People are often indecisive because they don't want criticism if things turn out badly. This fear comes from the same insecurity that causes us to remain silent and not make ourselves known.

It's precisely those times when we face a difficult choice that we must speak up and make a decision. Even if it's choosing between painful alternatives, it's almost always better to make a conscious choice and focus our efforts on making things work out as best they can, rather than make no decision at all. Make a decision and then make it right.

Then once a decision is made, do not revisit the choice endlessly. That can lead to regret, wasted energy, and worry, all of which are counterproductive. It's always good to review decisions from time-to-time to insure we want to continue down the same path or see if we want to make changes. In those circumstances, the focus is on the future, not the past. Don't fall into the trap of beating yourself or others up for making an honest decision. It does no one any good and can only cause reluctance to make decisions later.

Remember, decisions can lead to opportunities. My decision to apply to Air Force officer training when I was 18 was one of the biggest decisions of my life and it worked out wonderfully, yet it was not an easy decision to make. I was committing myself to join the military, almost certainly far from home, for at least the next 10 years.

The military had a very mixed reputation at the end of the Vietnam War in 1973. In Berkeley, where I would be going to college, students and non-students often had a negative reaction to people in the military. Ten years is a long time to an 18-year-old high school senior. What if I wasn't successful? What if I didn't like it? I had an idea what I was getting in to and I knew it wasn't all rosy. Still, the adventure and excitement and the opportunity to become a pilot called me. If I hesitated because I feared making a wrong decision, the chance for all of this would have passed me by. I made my decision. I made myself known.

For me, taking a chance and joining the Air Force was making a decision in a positive direction. It has been just as important for me to make a conscious decision when faced with difficult alternatives. When confronted with Carol's behavior at that restaurant in Colorado in 1983, I felt I faced two bad alternatives. I could continue in the marriage, knowing Carol was unhappy being my wife and didn't want to seek help, or I could file for divorce. Both alternatives were terrible, but it would have been far easier for me to not do anything. Just let things continue and hope something would happen.

This would have been "deciding not to decide." It would have relieved me of having to admit to my family and the world our marriage of two years had failed. It would have also allowed me to continue going to school at night, fulfill my commitment as a squadron scheduler, and improve my flying skills as a new KC-10 pilot without having to deal with a miserable and time-consuming divorce.

Even though I knew it would be publicly embarrassing, my life would be in an uproar, and the next year would be agonizing, I made a conscious decision to file for divorce. As difficult as that was, if I had not taken that painful step, my life would have been radically different — and much worse.

If you're looking for two guideposts to leading a purposeful life, it's important to speak up. Make yourself known. Tell people what you think. Then make a decision. Have the courage to decide — you'll be glad you did.

Chapter 37

Play

My grandsons Tom and Dane at Disneyland in 2018.
They remind us how important it is to play.

Just play. Have fun. Enjoy the game.

Michael Jordan, professional basketball player

Taking the time to play is important. Play allows us to take a break from our professional and personal responsibilities. It allows us time to focus on something we enjoy. It gives us an opportunity to interact with friends, family, or even work colleagues in an environment that doesn't demand we produce anything of value, except the experience. If we don't take time to recharge our batteries through play, we won't have the energy to do all the other things we want to do in life.

When we think of play, we often think of games or sports, but play could mean things as diverse as collecting stamps, tossing a football, reading a book, or mountain climbing. The important thing is we engage in an activity we enjoy. It doesn't have to be physical; although there's a lot of benefit in exercise.

I found in the military and in the corporate world that play was sometimes seen as frivolous and unproductive. In the Air Force, there was an expectation all of us had to keep in shape — they even required us to pass a physical fitness test every year. At the same time, the ongoing mission demanded us to put in long hours and even go on a 7-day/week work schedule when we deployed. Whether at home station or not, it was rare to have any scheduled group physical activity. We needed to make time to exercise, unless our job provided sufficient physical effort.

In my case, my duties as a pilot involved physical activity, but it wasn't strenuous enough to qualify as exercise. In fact, it involved hours of sitting. Given those circumstances, I found I needed to exercise (in my case, I run) or focus on something non-work-related just to relieve stress and keep myself sane. While it would have been so much easier to ignore my play needs, I made a point of prioritizing those activities in my schedule.

While I didn't deploy anywhere as a corporate program manager, I carried over that discipline when I transitioned to a long-hours job in the defense industry after my Air Force retirement. It worked out well, as I have continued to run (even marathons) into my 60s. I also enjoy reading history and I'm a big baseball fan. I love visiting with friends and traveling with JoAnn. We love to take walks wherever we are.

All of us need to take care of ourselves by incorporating play in our lives. Make it a priority in your life. You do yourself and others a great disservice if you aren't present for them at home, at work, and during your off hours. The only way you can keep yourself fully engaged over the long term is to identify what type of play you enjoy and take time to participate. Have fun.

Chapter 38

Objectives and Goals

The Warner Robins Chamber of Commerce presenting its
2001 Community Service Award to the 19th Air Refueling Group.
I am accepting the award on behalf of the Black Knights.
This was the first time we ever won this prestigious award and
it was the result of an enormous amount of successful effort by the members
of my group towards achieving this goal. (U.S. Air Force)

"Setting goals is the first step in turning the invisible into the visible."

Tony Robbins, American author, entrepreneur,
philanthropist, and life coach

It's important for us to know what we want to do and where we want to go. The only way to do that is to set goals and objectives. To clarify the difference between the two, a goal is a description of where we want to be and what we want to achieve — a destination. An objective is a measure of the progress we need to make to get to our goal/destination. Goals don't have to be grand "Climb Mount Everest" aspirations, although they can be if that's what we want. The important thing is to think about what we want and where we'd like to be one, two, five, even 10 years from now or longer. Once we decide on where we want to go, we can look at what it would take to get there.

There's a wealth of detailed literature on constructing good goals and objectives. Much of the advice centers on creating them in a SMART (Specific, Measurable, Achievable, Relevant, and Time-oriented) format. We want our goals to be things we strive to achieve and that inspire us. If they're too easy to attain or if they're not anything we care about, why bother?

The objectives we create lead to realizing our goals. Objectives are milestones we can use to track our progress, which is why we want them to be measurable and why we want a date attached. Without measurable objectives with assigned completion dates, we're not sure how far we've advanced. They can just continue forever without holding ourselves accountable for their accomplishment.

I want to emphasize how important it is to forgive yourself throughout this process. I find people are often much too hard on themselves if they feel they're not making fast enough progress. Don't beat yourself up if you feel you're falling short of what you want to achieve. You may find your original goal was too ambitious, or maybe you didn't even want to go there in the first place. If that's where you find yourself, you can sit down, reconsider your situation, and set new goals and objectives. Worrying or being discouraged with yourself is a complete waste of time.

We all know wonderful friends and family members who are talented, intelligent, and hard-working, but aren't really getting what they want out of life. It's often not a lack of desire or effort holding them back — it's a lack of focus. You can see them putting in lots of time and energy into life, but they're just spinning their wheels and getting nowhere. Creating goals and supporting objectives can help you make progress. The clarity they can give you is amazing. Goals and objectives also provide a basis for action. They are the first steps towards making the life you want a reality.

I've created many goals in my life: to be happily married to a loving wife; to raise happy and healthy children; to become an Air Force pilot; to graduate from the University of California with my bachelor's degree; etc., etc. If I hadn't created these goals and taken concrete actions toward achieving my objectives in support of these goals, none of them would have become a reality.

Even today, at 64, I have goals and objectives. I travel with my beautiful wife and we make seeing our children and grandchildren a priority. To better understand my post-Air Force work requirements, I continue my academic studies, recently earning an associate degree in computer science from community college at night. I have financial freedom through managing my money and continuing to earn more. I also train for and run one marathon each year.

My writing this book has been a goal of mine for years. It was only when I turned my desire into concrete objectives and took action to achieve those objectives that this became a reality.

If you want to be happy and successful, have faith in yourself. Set objectives and goals. Give yourself direction and make them happen.

Chapter 39

Inspiration

JoAnn and me after I completed the Las Vegas Rock 'n' Roll Marathon in 2009. Like many good things in life, training for and running a marathon requires inspiration.

"Just don't give up trying to do what you really want to do. Where there is love and inspiration, I don't think you can go wrong."

Ella Fitzgerald, American jazz singer

My life has shown me it's important to act from a feeling of inspiration. Inspired action is the next step toward achieving the goals and objectives I wrote about in the last chapter. When we do, it excites us. When we are inspired, we lift ourselves up. Meanwhile, we increase our energy and reinforce our positive outlook on life.

Our inspiration doesn't have to be our job, although that's wonderful if you've matched yourself up with what inspires you as your profession. Inspiration can come from a hobby or some other passionate interest. I recommend determining what interests you and find out more about it. Become an expert. Feel good about who you are and what you do. Give yourself the gift of getting up each morning and looking forward to what the day brings.

It's obvious I enjoyed being an Air Force pilot and officer. I loved what I was doing, and I felt my efforts were contributing toward something bigger and more important than just myself. I was helping to serve and protect my country, which meant a great deal to me. It was inspiring. Yet, I drew more inspiration from the wonderful men and women I worked with than anything else.

However, not everything was sunshine and roses. Over my 30 years in the Air Force, there were times when my job itself was decidedly less than inspiring.

On the 110+ degree Saudi Arabian afternoon in 1986 when our relief crews on the inbound KC-10 told me the squadron couldn't find an available aircraft commander to replace me and I would have to remain deployed there for yet another month, I wasn't feeling particularly inspired. I would have to cancel my long-scheduled vacation back home.

On the bitterly cold North Dakota night in 1998 as I stood on the Grand Forks Air Force Base parking ramp in the middle of a blizzard, I wasn't feeling too excited, either. I was trying to coordinate my aircrews and maintenance troops as they launched on a no-notice deployment to the Middle East in response to Saddam Hussein's latest saber-rattling. I could see the disappointment in the faces of the men and women I commanded; they knew they would be gone over Christmas. Yet, on these and countless other times during my career, I found inspiration in the brilliant, talented, and selfless professionals I had the privilege to work with. This was especially true during those times that were the most difficult.

To this day, two of my biggest interests are baseball and learning about history. I also love long-distance running. None of these activities are work-related, yet they bring me inspiration and joy. Writing this book and speaking to groups inspires me, too.

If you are searching for your inspiration, there are ways to help you discover it. Be open to new experiences and people. When you find delight or fascination, follow it. Most of all, don't be afraid to take chances. Focus on the positive. Imagine the best possible outcome and visualize that happening to you. Go where your heart leads you, knowing that those who love you will support and encourage you. Joy awaits.

Chapter 40

Nurture

This is a picture of my good friend Dave Swenson and me in Hawaii in 2015. Dave is an Alaska Airlines captain and he was on layover in Maui when JoAnn and I were living there. I have known Dave for over 40 years – we were pilots together at my first assignment in Michigan and then in California after that. Our friendship is a great example of the strong bonds people make in a healthy, nurturing environment, such as the Air Force.

"Management is about arranging and telling. Leadership is about nurturing and enhancing."

Tom Peters, American writer on business management practices

When I joined the Air Force, I had no intention of making it a career. I planned to do my best, but I expected to fulfill my six-year commitment from pilot training and then go fly for the airlines. This was emphatically true once the Air Force assigned me to a remote base in the frigid Upper Peninsula of Michigan after graduation from pilot training. For this California boy, I felt I might as well have been going to the surface of the moon.

Ironically, I was an unwitting contributor to my getting this undesirable assignment. The instructors at Reese AFB wanted me to come back and join them as a T-38 instructor. This was quite an honor, and I appreciated it; however, I had other desires. I wanted to fly large transport aircraft and see the world — and I said as much on my assignment request form. Years later, during my tour as an assignments officer in Nebraska, I understood what I was doing by submitting that assignment request was broadcasting my desire to get trained in flying large, airliner-type aircraft and then get hired by United or American Airlines.

What I soon discovered in Michigan was a nurturing, inclusive culture. What could have been a cold, lonely, three-year tour was instead one of the best times of my life. My squadron-mates went out of their way to get to know me and make me feel welcome. Senior officers took time to show me the ropes. I learned from some outstanding mentors and my near peers — they helped guide me toward what I needed to do to become competitive for promotion and find myself in rewarding assignments. They readily shared their wisdom and experience with me. They nurtured me along as a young officer. When I became more senior, I did the same for younger officers. This was a common experience I had throughout my career in the Air Force and it shows the power of being nurturing and inclusive. This power is available to all of us.

As you might expect, "nurture" is not a typical association people make with the military, yet I believe one of the great strengths of the Air Force was how we cared for each other. We didn't call it nurturing, we referred to it as mentoring, camaraderie, and esprit de corps. The same is true for all of us. While none of us is responsible for anyone else's behavior, it's important to take care of each other. This is especially true if we are parents or in leadership positions — our impact is very strong in these critical roles. Nurturing is important even if we only want to be a good friend.

We can tap into nurturing daily by welcoming the new person at work or the new neighbor who just moved in, even if they don't look like us or go to a different church or synagogue or mosque. Get to know them. Be courageous. Don't be afraid to allow yourself to be nurtured, either. We all want it and need it. Nurturing provides strength to get through difficult situations. None of us is an island.

Chapter 41

Trust

Chris, Emily, me, JoAnn, Dane, Jeanette, Justin, and Tom on a wonderful family vacation in Hawaii in 2014. Trusting in others and trusting in ourselves is important for leading a joyful life.

"The best way to find out if you can trust somebody is to trust them."

Ernest Hemingway, American novelist, short story writer, and journalist

As I described in Part 4 of this book, trust has been a very important part of my life. I wouldn't have had any success in my life without it.

I trusted in myself. I trusted that my decision to go into the Air Force would work out. I trusted my piloting skills would carry me through difficult flying situations. I trusted my leadership skills would help me navigate whatever challenges might arise.

I trusted other people. I trusted my Air Force leaders would look out for me. I trusted my fellow crewmembers would perform their jobs to the best of their abilities. I trusted my wife, JoAnn, would be honest and caring and loving.

I trusted my higher power would take care of me and help lead me to what was best. I trusted everything would work out.

Without question, all these things came to pass and more.

One key to success in life is knowing people are inherently trustworthy. I firmly believe this. We want to trust others and they want to trust us it's human nature. If we go through life trusting people as a matter of course, we will rarely be disappointed. On those few occasions when we run across someone who might take advantage of our faith and honesty, we can use it as a learning experience, much as I did with my ex-wife. Eventually, we find we don't attract untrustworthy people into our lives. Our paths just never intersect with theirs. Along with that, I personally found trust in a higher spirit is critical. I don't believe any religion, spiritual belief, or even a lack of religious belief is wrong. They're just different viewpoints on the same picture.

Chapter 42

Looking Ahead

Aim Point LLC — "Find Your Aim Point" — dedicated to helping people reinvent themselves through reconnecting with values and principles important to them.

The eight Aim Point principles I've described have been important for me throughout my life. They've helped me to maintain focus when confronted with important, often difficult decisions. Reconnecting with these principles has been critical when I've felt the need to reinvent myself. Once I've made this reconnection, I've found it so much easier to take inspired, meaningful action in pursuit of my desires.

If you find yourself in need of reinvention, I encourage you to take time, dig deep, reconnect with your values, and explore what inspires you ... what excites you. Without taking these critical first steps, you'll risk building your future on an unstable foundation. Uninspired action, no matter how well intended, is sooner or later headed for failure.

Where in your life have you almost crashed and burned (or choked), only to find yourself stronger and more courageous than ever? That is reinvention, and you've all done it. Reinvention is a fact of life these days. Just like my aim point on the runway, your aim point in life is up to you.

What are your intentions? What is your aim point? Is it time to reinvent yourself? If it is time, be confident of your success — you can do it. And you don't have to do it alone. There are those of us who can help.

I have truly enjoyed sharing my life journey and lessons learned with you. I hope I have given you something to think about. I also hope we have the opportunity to discuss this in more detail as time goes on. One of the most enjoyable parts of my career were those times when I've been able to mentor men and women, inside and outside of the military, throughout my life. I look forward to hearing from you as you find and follow your aim point. I invite you to reach out to me via email at colbrucehurd@gmail.com, follow me on Facebook at Col Bruce Hurd, and visit my webpage at www.colbrucehurd.com.

Appendix A

My Timeline and Background Information

Because I had 16 separate assignments in the Air Force and I jumped around my timeline as I wrote this book, I've gathered a summary of my duty history and associated background information to use as a reference to help clear up any confusion. These entries focus on where I was, when I was there, and what I was doing during each assignment or phase of my life. I've also identified key events on this timeline that I described as part of my book.

My wonderful brothers and sister in the mid-1960s.
Clockwise from upper left: Dave, Caroline, Kevin (in front of Caroline), Drew
(seated in chair), and me (on floor in front of Dave)

My wonderful siblings at Emily's and Chris's wedding in 2018.
From left to right: me, Dave, the bride and groom, Kevin,
Caroline, and Drew

From December 1954 to September 1973 I lived in the San Francisco Bay Area with my father, mother, and siblings Dave, Caroline, Drew, and Kevin — I was between Drew and Kevin and we were all close in age, with just seven years between the youngest and oldest. Something of a mob scene. We lived in a nice suburban house in Los Altos in northwestern Santa Clara Valley before it became "The Silicon Valley." It was semi-agricultural then, where it wasn't unusual to be driving along the main roads and see small shopping centers, houses, and orchards all on the same block.

I went to Grant Elementary School and Cupertino Junior High School and I graduated from Homestead High School in 1973. I played a lot of football and baseball and I was a Boy Scout for a while. Where I excelled, though, was when I became a YMCA camp counselor during the summer after my sophomore year. In addition to getting leadership experience during the summer, I became involved with the high school age "Hi-Y" program of the Northwest YMCA. Hi-Y was a social/service club aimed at high school boys and girls.

At the beginning of my junior year, I started a club with my friends from Homestead and they elected me president since I was the one guy all of them knew. I really enjoyed it and I was elected president of the entire 12-club Northwest YMCA Hi-Y council my senior year. In addition to being a lot of fun, I'm certain being elected to the presidency of a large, multi-school service organization helped me get admitted to the University of California, Berkeley and get awarded an Air Force ROTC scholarship. *This was when there were lots of incidents with my Mom's drinking. This was also when my 6th Grade teacher's abuse happened in 1966.*

<u>From September 1973 to April 1977</u> I was a student at the UC Berkeley and an Air Force ROTC cadet. I started off as a physical science major. After one year of beating my head against the wall trying to compete with pre-med students, I realized I would be wise to switch my major to something a little more up my alley. I applied for and was accepted to the upper division School of Business Administration (now known as the Haas School of Business). Much better.

I graduated in April 1977, one quarter short of four years because my father had the wisdom to encourage me to take the College Level Examination Program (CLEP) tests before starting classes, for which I received 30 units of quarter credit. These credits didn't allow me to get out of taking any courses I needed for graduation. What they did was allow me to not have to take classes solely to meet the total 180-credit requirement for a bachelor's degree. For the 10 months between college and the Air Force, I did some travelling, and I worked as a pizza delivery driver. I also worked as a "die inventory clerk" at a new company called Intel in Santa Clara. *This was when my Mom first went to rehab in 1975. This was also when the Air Force cut the number of pilot training candidates by 70% in 1976. Right before graduation, I also had the precommissioning eyesight exam prior to getting assigned to pilot training.*

Air Force Timeline

From January - December 1978 I was a Student Pilot in Air Force Undergraduate Pilot Training (UPT), at Reese AFB, just outside of Lubbock, Texas. UPT was conducted by the 64th Flying Training Wing (64 FTW) and I was in Class 79-02 (our patch pictured above). The year-long UPT program was separated into two phases, primary and advanced, each lasting about six months. The primary trainer was the subsonic Cessna T-37 "Tweet" twin-engine jet. At Reese, the 35th Flying Training Squadron (35 FTS) conducted that phase. The advanced trainer was the supersonic Northrop T-38 "Talon" and the 54 FTS ran that phase of training at Reese.

All pilot trainees had to go through the entire training program regardless of whether the newly graduated pilot ended up in heavies (tankers, airlifters, or bombers), fighters, or trainers (new pilots assigned as UPT instructors). The training objective was to create a universally assignable pilot who could transfer between aircraft types based upon the needs of the Air Force. In practice, pilots almost never made the move between heavies and fighters once they became fully mission-ready.

Recognizing this reality, the Air Force modified UPT in later years to focus on mastering specific skillsets needed by tanker/airlift pilots (such as crew coordination/management) or fighter/bomber pilots (such as tactical maneuvering). Pilots were assigned to an airlift/tanker or fighter/bomber track after the basic flying training phase. In 1978, though, all of us had to master every skill, including multi-ship fingertip formation flying and tactical map navigation — skills that were not required during my flying career as a tanker pilot. ***This was when I had my nearly fatal T-38*** *night flight and my failed T-37 Mid-Phase Check. Ultimately, the entire experience was very successful.*

From January - May 1979 I was a KC-135 student copilot at Castle AFB, near Merced, California. KC-135 qualification training was conducted by Strategic Air Command's (SAC's) Combat Crew Training School (CCTS). The initial, academic part of CCTS was the responsibility of the instructors of the 4017th Combat Crew Training Squadron. Flight training was conducted by the instructor pilots, navigators, and boom operators of the 93rd Air Refueling Squadron. Both organizations were part of the historic 93rd Bombardment Wing. After four months of academic and flight training, I graduated as a qualified KC-135 copilot, ready to move onto my first operational assignment in Northern Michigan.

The focus was on getting us to succeed. The CCTS schedule was leisurely enough, so I had weekends off unless something big was happening on Monday. Castle was also only two hours from where I grew up and I took advantage of that by going home to see family and friends from Friday after class to Sunday night — it was great. Most importantly, this was not a situation like UPT where we students were always on the edge of failing out.

Until I became mission qualified, I was still considered a student; however, CCTS instructors treated students like qualified professionals, with an appropriate level of respect provided. CCTS was demanding, but it was a nice surprise to be taught by instructors proud to be tanker pilots.

This was quite different from what we were led to believe SAC would be like while we were students at UPT.

After graduating from CCTS and before reporting to KI Sawyer AFB, *I went to Land Survival Training (with the mock POW camp) at Fairchild AFB in Washington and Water Survival Training at Homestead AFB in Florida.*

From June 1979 - August 1982 I flew the KC-135A for the 46th Air Refueling Squadron (ARS) at KI Sawyer AFB, just south of Marquette in the Upper Peninsula of Michigan. I began my assignment in the 46th as a copilot, and as soon as I acquired the minimum number of hours to qualify, I upgraded to aircraft commander at Castle AFB in early 1982. The moment when I received command responsibility for my very own KC-135 aircraft and crew was a proud and humbling point in my career.

The 46 ARS, along with the 644th Bombardment Squadron (flying B-52s) was one of two operational squadrons in the 410th Bombardment Wing (BMW) at KI Sawyer. While there was a separate F-106 squadron flying an air defense mission, all other base units and activities were designed to support the bomb wing. With 21 assigned crews, the 46th was one of the largest KC-135 squadrons in SAC. In 1979, the Boeing KC-135A was the backbone of the SAC refueling fleet, with over 600 aircraft in the inventory. The "A" model, with its loud, water-injected Pratt & Whitney J57 engines, was seriously underpowered when it was fully loaded with fuel.

This performance challenge caused the Air Force to build enormous 2 ½ mile runways so both the KC-135 and B-52 would have enough distance to accelerate to takeoff speed at full weight (such as when we were on alert). The takeoffs I most remember from my A-model days were the ones involving either heavyweight fuel loads or Minimum Interval Takeoff (MITO) operations designed for "flush launch" of the alert force. Both situations required very precise takeoff calculations and timing even if everything went right. If there were engine problems or water injection was lost close to "committed to takeoff" speed, the degree of difficulty/danger and the need for quick, appropriate reactions increased exponentially.

While we trained for worst-case situations, I thankfully never had either of these takeoff emergencies occur. I did have MITOs where I was uncomfortably close to the aircraft in front of me (due to differences in acceleration) and heavyweight takeoffs where I used every bit of the runway to lumber my fully loaded plane into the air, barely clearing the trees just past the end of the runway.

I recall one time when we scared the crap out of a motorcycle rider on the base perimeter road. We happened to fly over him as we took off heavyweight on an unexpectedly hot August day in Upper Michigan. He emerged from a row of trees and did a head-snapping double take as it became clear our paths were intersecting — his eyes became huge as he saw us coming. We couldn't have cleared him by more than 10 feet. We even checked afterward to make sure there wasn't an accident caused by our jet blast.

This was where I met and married my first wife Carol. It was also where we had the incident with my mother taking bottles of alcohol from the distinguished visitor quarters. Also, it was during this assignment my squadron commander stood up during an inspection debrief and confronted the SAC Inspector General for unwarranted remarks aimed at us in his squadron — I've always admired him for that.

From August 1982 - September 1984 I flew the KC-10 for the 9th Air Refueling Squadron at March AFB, near Riverside, California. It thrilled me when Strategic Air Command chose me to become a KC-10 copilot in the spring of 1982, shortly after I upgraded to KC-135 aircraft commander (pilot-in-command). The KC-10s were just starting to come off the assembly line, and I was a part of a brand-new squadron being started from scratch with handpicked, highly experienced crewmembers selected from throughout SAC. It was exciting, and I felt like I was a part of something special.

The McDonnell Douglas KC-10 Extender is the military version of the three-engine DC-10 airliner. The KC-10 is much larger and more versatile than the KC-135. The biggest improvements are its capability to receive fuel midair as well as carry large amounts of cargo. The Air Force developed the KC-10 to supplement the KC-135 following Air Force air refueling experiences in Southeast Asia and the Middle East. Only 60 KC-10s were produced for the Air Force, so those of us who flew the plane got to know each other well over the years. The working environment was fantastic — I enjoyed the mission and the people I worked with. I made some of the best friends I had in the Air Force during this two-year assignment. This exciting, leading-edge experience was a big reason I decided to make the Air Force a career.

In addition to developing my skills as a KC-10 pilot during this time, I volunteered to be a squadron scheduler — a full-time staff role for a one-year period that would help me better understand how the squadron functions and provide greater visibility for me in a highly competitive environment. I also earned my master's degree in systems management from the University of Southern California at night. *It was during this time Carol and I divorced. I filed for divorce in early 1983, with the divorce becoming finalized in mid-1984. It's also when I had to rush to my parents' home from work to see if Mom was okay after a severe drinking bout.*

From September 1984 - September 1985 I was assigned to the Air Staff Training (ASTRA) program at the Pentagon. ASTRA was a yearlong tour of duty designed to expose young officers to air staff operations at Air Force Headquarters. Each year, the Air Force chose 75 young captains at around five or six years of service for this career-broadening experience, where we were introduced to high-level Air Force leadership perspectives. We also participated in other educational opportunities while we worked as staff officers within a headquarters directorate.

At the conclusion of the tour, we were sent back to our primary career fields to continue our careers. This was an extraordinary experience for me and I appreciated the opportunity to take part. During this time, I spent six months as Assistant Military Airlift Command Liaison Officer to the Joint Chiefs of Staff, and six months as an action officer in the HQ USAF Directorate of Personnel Programs. *This was where I worked for the colonel who had integrity issues — a good example of a bad leader.*

From September 1985 - January 1988 I flew the KC-10 as an aircraft commander and instructor pilot for the 32d Air Refueling Squadron at Barksdale AFB, near Shreveport, Louisiana. Along with having my own assigned crew, I also served as a flight commander for three additional crews. The 32 ARS was one of three flying squadrons in the 2d Bombardment Wing, along with the 20th Bombardment Squadron (B-52) and the 71st Air Refueling Squadron (KC-135). With three active operational squadrons flying three different types of aircraft, the 2d Bomb Wing was one of the largest flying wings in the Air Force.

This was one of my most fun assignments: I was a full-time aircraft commander/instructor pilot and my flying skills were at their peak. I enjoyed leading my crew and the feeling of being good at what I do. Because of our squadron's worldwide commitments, I spent a great deal of time flying challenging missions throughout Europe and the Middle East. As one of the few unmarried aircraft commanders in the squadron, I deployed regularly to Saudi Arabia, often on short notice.

Our squadron had a standing obligation to station three crews and two aircraft at Riyadh Air Base when the U.S. presence in the Middle East was very limited. Most of our missions revolved around refueling the USAF E-3A Airborne Warning and Control System (AWACS) aircraft and Royal Saudi Air Force F-15s in support of their air defense mission. The Iran-Iraq War was raging at the time and Iran was just across the Persian Gulf from Saudi Arabia. Saudi Arabia was a very prominent Iraq supporter, and they were concerned Iran might attack them. It was only a few years afterward that things would turn around dramatically. Iraq invaded Kuwait in the summer of 1990 and Saudi Arabia would develop into a major staging base for the 1991 American-led invasion of Iraq during the Gulf War.

I am grateful for all the success I had at Barksdale. In addition to making wonderful friends throughout my tour, I upgraded to KC-10 instructor pilot, and I was promoted early to major in late 1986. The Air Force also selected me to attend the prestigious Army Command and Staff College, which would happen in 1990. Plus, the Cajun food in Louisiana is fantastic. *This was where I became qualified in night air refueling on that wild training flight. I also flew home for Christmas and Mom entered rehab for the last time in 1986. She finally stopped drinking during this timeframe, too. It was also during this assignment that I had the privilege of working for Lt Col Lias, my squadron commander — an outstanding leadership example.*

From January 1988 - June 1990, I served as a staff officer at Strategic Air Command Headquarters at Offutt AFB, near Omaha, Nebraska. I became an assignments officer, working as the Deputy Chief of Selective and Command Assignments, followed by a move up to become Chief of Tanker Assignments. Both jobs were non-flying positions, and I missed the excitement and satisfaction of being a pilot and leading a crew. That said, I worked with a great group of men and women performing an often thankless job of managing the assignments of SAC aircrew officers (pilots and navigators).

I also learned a great deal about how SAC and the Air Force manage people — this knowledge would be useful for mentoring younger officers as I moved into leadership positions later in my career. As I officially became a major in early 1988 (having been selected for promotion at the end of 1986) and saw things from the vantage point of a fully embedded headquarters staff officer, this was the first time I embraced things from a much broader, command-wide viewpoint, rather than just seeing the situation from the limited perspective of a line pilot within a flying squadron. This was no coincidence, as the Air Force encourages mid-level officers to complete a headquarters staff tour such as I did at SAC. It's almost a requirement for an officer to have this type of assignment to be a viable candidate for promotion to lieutenant colonel and beyond. There was often fierce competition for these types of jobs.

One huge benefit of this job was the regular schedule I had. I went to work and came home at the same time each day, travel was infrequent, and I had most weekends off. It was great. This was very different from the "don't plan on anything, always be ready to deploy, and fly at all hours of the day and night" life of a KC-10 crewmember. It was also different from the one week out of three scheduled exile of an alert-pulling KC-135 pilot.

My schedule at SAC Headquarters allowed me to have a semi-normal social life since I had the ability to arrange a date with a woman and expect to make it. *It was during this assignment I met and married my wife JoAnn.* We connected in the summer of 1988 via a video dating service named "New Beginnings." JoAnn had been divorced for some time and she supported herself and her son Justin by working as a registered nurse. We became engaged around one year after that. *It was shortly after we were engaged when the doctor told me I would never be able to father a child. It was also when we started our subsequent search for medical assistance. This was also where I worked for the colonel who was an extreme careerist — so much so that he lost the trust and respect of many of us who worked for him.*

From June 1990 - June 1991 I was a student at the U.S. Army Command and General Staff College (CGSC) at Fort Leavenworth, Kansas just outside of Kansas City. Selection to attend CGSC was considered a real plus for an officer, as we represented the Air Force to the Army's upcoming leaders — they wanted to ensure we left a favorable impression as capable and intelligent. Because I was the only Air Force officer in my staff group of 14 majors (all the rest being Army, of course), I needed to speak on all things Air Force, not just tanker operations. This assignment forced me to learn more about my military branch, which helped make me an even more well-rounded Air Force officer.

This assignment was great in so many ways. I've always enjoyed learning, and this was an opportunity to study a wide variety of military history and national security topics as a full-time student for a year. The civilian and military professors at CGSC were outstanding and the resources and guest speakers available to us as students were tremendous. I also liked interacting with my talented and dedicated Army classmates, marveling at all they have to do to accomplish their challenging mission.

This year was also a time of change for the three of us (JoAnn, Justin, and me), as we merged as a family for the first time. Since we were scheduled to move at the end of our first six months of marriage, we never consolidated everything we had while we were in Omaha — we still had two rental homes full of furniture and clothes. The move went well, with a lot of the credit going to Justin as he adapted to a new step-dad and a move

away from his friends in Omaha. *__The absolute highlight of this assignment__*
__was JoAnn becoming pregnant with Emily.__

__From June 1991 - May 1994__ I was Assistant Operations Officer and,
later, Operations Officer for the 344th Air Refueling Squadron at Seymour
Johnson AFB, near Goldsboro, North Carolina. The 344th was one of two
KC-10 squadrons in a huge composite wing that also included three F-15E
fighter squadrons and an operational support squadron. I was back flying as
a KC-10 instructor pilot, which was very rewarding in itself.

I also assumed my first major leadership role as the operations officer
in the 344th — it was a huge step up. In that role I was second-in-command
of the 200+ men and women of the squadron, and I oversaw all flying
operations and aircrews. It was an enormous increase in responsibility, and
I was honored to be selected by the wing commander to take on this job.

During my time as operations officer, I deployed with our Seymour
Johnson KC-10s to Al Dhafra Air Base near Abu Dhabi in the United
Arab Emirates (UAE) for close to two months in the summer of 1993.
While deployed, we supported Operation Southern Watch operations by
air refueling Air Force and Navy fighters and E-3 Airborne Warning and
Control (AWACS) aircraft patrolling the no-fly zone over Iraq. I also
performed as squadron commander for three months while my boss was in
the UAE in the fall of 1993.

My tour as operations officer, which included directing flying operations
in the UAE and acting as squadron commander when my boss was deployed,

was an exciting highlight of my career. I had the amazing opportunity to mentor and lead the wonderful men and women under my charge. I also had the very good fortune of being promoted to lieutenant colonel during this tour.

Emily was born in July 1991, shortly after we arrived in North Carolina. Emily's miracle birth, along with my marriage to JoAnn and gaining Justin as my bonus son, are the two highlights of my entire life. Nothing can compare to those events. This is also where I confronted the married captain about his inappropriate behavior with the female airmen while deployed to the UAE.

From May 1994 - July 1995 I was Commander of the 6th Air Refueling Squadron (6 ARS) at March AFB, near Riverside, California. The 6 ARS was one of two flying squadrons (the other being my old 9th Air Refueling Squadron) in the 722d Air Refueling Wing (722 ARW). Becoming a squadron commander is the goal of nearly all flying officers in the Air Force — it represents a career achievement for those of us fortunate enough to be given a command. I was indeed very privileged Air Mobility Command chose me as commander of the 6 ARS.

In this role, I commanded a KC-10 unit, and this was the only time the Air Force ever assigned me to a location where I had lived before. I was one of the first pilots assigned to KC-10s at March in 1982 when we started the 9 ARS, and in my role as commander, I would be shutting down the 6 ARS as the unit moved from March to Travis AFB in Northern California.

The squadron move occurred because the Air Force was downsizing and consolidating. March was closing as an active duty base due to congressional Base Realignment and Closure decisions; however, March remains open as an Air Force Reserve base even today.

There's nothing like being an Air Force squadron commander; I enjoyed it immensely. I had the chance to lead an amazing group of 200+ officers (mostly pilots), noncommissioned officers, and airmen. I also had excellent commanders above me who allowed me the freedom to lead my squadron how I felt best. I could use the experience I gained over my previous 16 years to help develop my officers and airmen individually and forge them into a high-performing team without excessive influence from above.

During my tenure, I deployed with my squadron to both Zimbabwe (for a short tenure in support of the Rwandan relief effort) and the UAE (for a four-month deployment, I was in command of the 4413th Air Refueling Squadron (Provisional) supporting Operation Southern Watch). The Southern Watch deployment was to Al Dhafra Air Base, the same location I had gone to a year-and-a-half earlier. Both deployments were very successful and highly rewarding, although the UAE deployment was more challenging this time around because of its length and the fact my troops and I were all facing family moves to other locations once we arrived back home to California — this weighed on all our minds.

I am proud to say the highly deserving and talented men and women of my squadron won several awards while I was in command. My maintenance section, which was more than half my squadron, won the Maintenance Effectiveness Award for being the "Best Large Aircraft Maintenance Unit" in the entire Air Force. Wow, that still blows me away — what a remarkable team of airmen I had the pleasure to lead. The 722 ARW also nominated my squadron to compete for the Spaatz Trophy as the best tanker squadron in the Air Force. I was also honored that the wing commander chose me as the 722 ARW nominee for the Air Force's Lance P. Sijan Award for outstanding leadership.

It was during this assignment when I had my one-way "shape up now" meeting with my squadron leadership. It's also when we had the sexual harassment incident with my executive officer and the yellow stripe painted on the back of one of my NCOs. Those two incidents happened while we were deployed to the UAE.

From July 1995 - June 1996 I was once again a student, this time at the Air War College (AWC) at Maxwell AFB, near Montgomery, Alabama. AWC is the senior professional military education school of the Air Force. The one-year course emphasizes the employment of air, space, and cyberspace in joint operations, with a focus on higher-level national security topics. AWC is intended for colonels and those lieutenant colonels seen as having great potential to be promoted to colonel. Officers from all four military services, career civil servants, and foreign military officers were all in attendance.

This was a fun year. After the around-the-clock stress associated with squadron command, it was a welcome relief to be part of a 12-officer seminar where I was simply responsible for participating in class, passing tests, and doing my required homework. I found the coursework fascinating, the professors extremely knowledgeable, and our class discussions lively and entertaining. The highlight of the school year was when we all travelled to different regions of the world as part of a two-week focused study where we interacted with our military and civilian counterparts in foreign countries. For this, we divided into nine groups — I was a part of the South America seminar, where we traveled to Brazil, Argentina, and Chile. The trip turned out to be fantastic — I enjoyed it immensely.

After returning, all of us wrote our dissertations on topics associated with our regional travel. My dissertation ("Free Trade in the Americas: Regional Trade Agreements as National Security Policy") dealt with the importance of trade agreements from a national security perspective. Trade agreements, such as the North American Free Trade Agreement (NAFTA) are often judged by the economic benefits they provide. I argued the national security benefits were just as great, since trade agreements enhance cooperation and increase stability for all participants. I was surprised and honored when the AWC faculty chose my dissertation as a finalist to compete for the 1996 Chairman of the Joint Chiefs of Staff National Defense and Military Strategic Essay Award. I hadn't envisioned myself as a distinguished scholar or author until that point.

From June 1996 - July 1998 I served as a Strategic Planner within the Directorate for Plans and Policy at the United States Atlantic Command (USACOM) in Norfolk, Virginia. While the overall commander of USACOM was a four-star Navy admiral, a two-star Air Force general led the plans directorate. USACOM was a joint service command responsible for the wartime control of all U.S. forces operating in the Atlantic and Caribbean region. It was a holdover from the Cold War days when we needed to be prepared to fight a major war against the Soviets where the Atlantic Theater would be a major focus for our naval forces.

Since the collapse of the USSR in 1991, though, Atlantic Command had focused primarily on the Caribbean with an emphasis on containing Cuba, dealing with unstable countries (such as Haiti), and preventing the flow of drugs into the U.S. from South America. When I arrived in 1996, USACOM was beginning a transformation into United States Joint Forces Command (USJFCOM). USJFCOM had a much larger role, controlling US-based military forces under a single joint commander. While it wasn't intended to have a specific combat mission, USJFCOM would be responsible for training and coordinating the deployment of all joint forces in support of the regional wartime commanders in Europe, the Pacific, the Middle East, South America, Africa, etc.

A primary purpose of my job was to help our admirals and generals develop a vision for the command as it moved into its new role. I worked with a talented team of Army, Marine, and Naval officers to make this happen (I was the only Air Force officer on the team and, hence, they looked to me for "the Air Force perspective"). It was fascinating to see the interplay between the four military services and the senior officers as they gave their perspectives and negotiated among themselves.

I also participated in some fascinating classified tabletop exercises involving information operations. These exercises were sophisticated for the time, but I'm certain they'd be considered rather primitive now (20+ years later). While I was only in this assignment for two years before the Air Force promoted me to colonel and pulled me back into the Air Force, I very much appreciate my wonderful friends at Atlantic Command and all I learned from my military comrades there.

From July 1998 - June 1999 I served as Deputy Commander for the 319th Operations Group within the 319th Air Refueling Wing at Grand Forks AFB in North Dakota. The 319th was one of three massive KC-135 tanker wings in the Air Force, and its operations group contained four fully manned squadrons of KC-135s and an operational support squadron — this was a result of the same Air Force-wide force structure consolidation that caused my old squadron at March AFB to move in 1995. I took a short requalification course in the KC-135 and joined the 319th in July 1998.

The KC-135 had changed a lot since I last flew it in 1982. The most notable difference was the new, much more powerful CFM-56 engines with twice as much thrust as the water-injection engines from years earlier. This allowed for larger fuel loads and operations from shorter runways. This difference was so significant, the re-engined KC-135s were re-designated KC-135R (as opposed to the original KC-135A model).

I enjoyed this assignment a lot. I was back in flying operations after three years away and, most especially, I was in a large Air Force wing focused on tanker operations. It was refreshing to be part of a team that wasn't considered an adjunct to B-52s or F-15Es. I saw some of this at March AFB in the 722d, but the 319th was much bigger and, as a result, carried a lot more weight. We also were very busy.

Between Saddam Hussein rattling his sword (where we would need to deploy/respond) and what turned out to be a major, months-long deployment to European air bases in support of the 1998-99 Kosovo War, we seemed to always be meeting ourselves coming and going. On many of those occasions where we needed to generate crews and aircraft for short-notice deployment, I filled the role as group commander when my boss was not on station or busy with other duties.

It was a high-stress operational environment. We often accomplished our mission in freezing cold and blizzard-like conditions. I learned a great deal, though. The dedicated and talented men and women of the 319th were ultimately very successful. I'm proud of them and honored to have served as their deputy commander (and sometimes acting commander).

From June 1999 - July 2001 I served as Commander of the 19th Air Refueling Group (ARG) at Robins AFB, outside Warner Robins, Georgia. While every one of my military assignments was enjoyable and special in their own way, this was the best and most rewarding job I ever had in the Air Force, along with my squadron command. The 19 ARG had 500+ personnel and was composed of four separate squadrons: the 99th Air Refueling Squadron (KC-135 aircrews), the 19th Aircraft Generation Squadron (KC-135 maintenance), the 19th Operations Support Squadron (intelligence, planning, standardization/evaluation, inspector general, and other support functions tied to KC-135 flying operations), and the 19th Maintenance Squadron (C-5 and C-141 depot maintenance at the air logistics complex on base).

I loved being the 19th commander. The men and women of the 19th were absolutely the best part, and the independent structure of this command lent to it being especially challenging and enjoyable. I was in charge of the only separate tanker group in the Air Force — meaning I didn't have a wing commander on base. My boss was a two- or three-star general at McGuire AFB in New Jersey, who had enormous responsibilities beyond my group. This meant I had more freedom to do what I felt was important. Without a senior officer in my chain-of-command above me on base, though, I was also held solely responsible for the success or failure of my group. This was exactly how I wanted it.

There were numerous challenges throughout my two years of group command, but I don't want to leave the impression being commander of the 19th was a burden, or I considered it unreasonably difficult — it wasn't, and I didn't. I had plenty of help from my outstanding squadron commanders and my superb staff. We managed to navigate through all of this and received tremendous recognition as well. During my tour as commander, in addition to being awarded the Air Force Outstanding Unit Award and the Spaatz Trophy twice, I was proud I could get recognition for the outstanding leadership displayed by several of my squadron commanders — they each did just an excellent job for me, their squadrons, and my group. I was also able to convince my boss many of my amazing noncommissioned officers and junior enlisted standouts deserved early promotions and other types of acknowledgement. This success in gaining recognition for my people was one of the most rewarding parts of my job.

This was where these leadership challenges I identified earlier occurred: *the shaming of a senior master sergeant who stuttered, the refusal of a young lieutenant to wear a flightsuit for religious reasons, the general-officer investigation for integrity issues regarding promotion recommendation forms, the temporary misplacement of a top secret document, the firing of a squadron commander for disobeying a direct order, my recommendation to court-martial a chief master sergeant, and the time I stood up for my two officers who were being scapegoated for an incident that happened in Hawaii. It was also when I trusted the Universe to get me the next assignment I wanted.*

From July 2001- July 2004 I was the Chief of the Programs and Mobility Division within the Logistics and Security Assistance Directorate of the United States European Command (USEUCOM) in Stuttgart, Germany. In this position I was responsible for all joint supply and transportation processes, plans, and programs that involved cooperation between the three major military services stationed in Europe: Army, Air Force, and Navy. There was only a tiny Marine presence in Europe, so they were represented by their Navy counterparts.

I had a staff of 20 experienced and talented officers and government civilians who worked for me as we tirelessly strove to improve the "en route" mobility infrastructure (typically airfields) and supply chain processes requiring multi-service cooperation within Europe. In addition to running the day-to-day operations for the division and providing an overarching vision to my staff, I collaborated with my Air Force, Army, and Navy counterparts to make things better for our soldiers, airmen, and sailors in Europe.

Of all the jobs I held during my Air Force career, I probably had the most system-wide impact in this position. I'm glad I held the position for three years, because it took that long to make progress in many areas. I found I had to wait out the retirement or transfer of some older, rather hidebound colonels I had to deal with to initiate necessary changes to make progress. In the end, I accomplished more during my last year than my first two years combined. It wasn't because I was working any harder. It was because I could cooperate with my new Army counterparts more effectively.

My staff and I had been working on a multitude of issues and plans that began to come to fruition near the end of my first two years. Because of our preparation, we were able to institute many of the process changes necessary to dramatically improve the speed and reduce the cost of transporting and delivering supplies to all our military locations throughout Europe. What made this even more impressive is that we accomplished all of this against the backdrop of the 9/11 attack and our subsequent supporting efforts for the War in Afghanistan (starting in October 2001) and Iraq War (which began ramping up in 2002).

Near the end of my tour, I was fortunate to be invited as one of the keynote speakers at the annual National Defense Transportation Association gathering in Germany. I felt very honored since I was the only presenter who was not a career military transportation officer. One of the most satisfying compliments I received during my European tour was when two Air Force senior NCOs came up to me at the conclusion of my three-year chairmanship of the quarterly European Theater Distribution Conference. I had worked closely with them the entire time I had been chairman. I was in my Air Force blue uniform that day. Typically, I wore my BDU camouflaged uniform, which was identical for all four military Services. The NCOs both expressed great surprise I was an Air Force officer. I worked very hard my entire tour to create an atmosphere of fairness and impartiality by not favoring the Air Force, the Army, or the Navy. The NCOs' reactions to finding out I was an Air Force officer, combined with our mutual successes over the three years I had been there, told me I had succeeded.

From July 2004 - June 2005 I was, once again, a student. This time, both JoAnn and I took the intense Basic French course at the Defense Language Institute (DLI) at the Presidio of Monterey in California. They sent me there to prepare for my follow-on assignment working with Belgian and Luxembourger senior military officers as a section chief supporting the U.S. ambassadors to Belgium and Luxembourg. In my new capacity, they deemed it essential that I learn French, which I wholeheartedly accepted. Because we, as a couple, had a representational role in Belgium, JoAnn could take the French course with me; consequently, we studied together and sat next to each other in class.

This was a fun assignment, and I loved living in Carmel, right next to the Bay Area where I grew up. The school was intense, with more written, oral, and listening examinations than any other course of study I've ever taken. Each day we would have about seven hours of class, with endless examinations of one type or another mixed in throughout the week. It was constant. Some exams were relatively small quizzes while many were major tests. And they all were graded, and they all had to be passed, which was a major contributor to the small 50 percent(!) graduation rate of our class.

Fifty percent was an about average success rate for DLI. The entire experience was numbing and the proliferation of tests contributed to the sense of always being under the gun — this feeling was especially pointed since I was the senior ranking officer at the school and the absolute last thing I wanted to do was report to my new boss (the American Ambassador to Belgium) and have to tell him I flunked French. JoAnn went through the entire course with me, including all the exams. In the end, both of us successfully graduated and I'm grateful I had the chance to learn this fascinating new language.

From July 2005 - August 2007, my last assignment in the Air Force, I worked directly for the U.S. Ambassador to Belgium as his Chief of the Office of Defense Cooperation (ODC) at the American Embassy in

Brussels. I also worked for the U.S. Ambassador to Luxembourg; although that role took up much less of my time, as Luxembourg only had a couple of small American facilities on their soil and supported an army of 1,000 (though they did use mostly American equipment). I had a small team of officers, American civilian employees, and Belgian nationals working for me in my capacity as section chief.

I received this assignment because the general who made it was the same person I reported to in my previous job at USEUCOM. When I found out the ODC Chief job in Belgium was coming open, I expressed an interest. My boss liked the job I was doing and had confidence in my ability to reinvent myself in this entirely new role. JoAnn, Emily, and I were interested in remaining in Europe and we looked forward to the exciting adventures we would have in this new location. We enjoyed it thoroughly. I loved the job, which not only required me to engage with high-ranking Belgian military officers, but also offered me the opportunity to work with Belgian government officials and Belgian defense industry representatives.

Additionally, NATO headquarters, an enormous organization, is in Brussels. As a result, I had the chance to connect with the many American defense industry representatives located there during my assignment. These connections would help me considerably as I began my search for a job following my 30-year military career. During my two-year tour, I organized a forum for all the Belgium-based American defense representatives, I chaired a panel on defense industry cooperation at our EUCOM-wide security assistance conference, and I facilitated the establishment of strong bonds between our U.S. ambassador and defense industry representatives in Brussels. What I'm most proud of, though, was my direct intervention between the USAF and Belgian Air Force to successfully negotiate the targeting pod contract I described earlier.

One of the aspects of my job in Belgium I found fascinating was the requirement to entertain senior Belgian officials and other officers I worked with. We would do this at our home just outside of Brussels — I even had a small and tightly controlled budget for that sort of thing. It was a real pleasure for JoAnn and me to get to know them and their spouses outside of official channels. It was particularly fun for us to gain an understanding of the "European way" of entertaining, which tends to be much more formalized, with distinct protocols associated with it. We also used this opportunity to introduce the Belgians to some of our American customs, such as when we held a traditional American Thanksgiving dinner for them.

A favorite memory of mine was Valentine's Day in 2007, when we hosted numerous generals and admirals and their spouses at our house for dinner. Afterwards, in the spirit of the holiday, we played a G-rated version of The Newlywed Game, wherein we separated the men and women and asked them questions about their spouses. We then gathered back together in our living room and asked their spouses the same questions to see how each of them thought the other one had responded.

To set the stage, Valentine's Day in Belgium is considered a private affair between a couple — certainly not an occasion for gathering to play a game about their relationships, so this was something radically different for everyone involved. Despite this extraordinary departure from what typically were rather scripted social events, the Belgians loved the game. They thought it was hilarious, especially because it gave them an opportunity to connect with other Belgian couples they may not have known well to begin with. While I don't remember anything monumental coming out of this or any other social events we hosted, JoAnn and I were very pleased to make such wonderful Belgian friends and to provide some fun for everyone involved. *This was when we bought our home in San Diego before I even had a firm job offer—another act of trust.*

Post-Air Force Timeline

From August 2007 to October 2015 I worked at Science Applications International Corporation (SAIC) as a Senior Program Manager. I started my job search while I was finishing my tour in Belgium, going on a job-hunting trip to San Diego and Southern California in April 2007. While I was in San Diego, I made some excellent contacts at SAIC and other companies in the area. In July, SAIC offered me a position, whereas other companies indicated they were on the verge, but nothing firm materialized. Being a big believer in "bird in the hand," I gratefully accepted the SAIC position and joined the company. I have been with SAIC or its renamed successor Leidos for the last 10+ years.

For my first six years at SAIC, I was the Program Director for the complex and classified Common User Application Software (CUAS) application — a key component of the Department of Defense Electronic Key Management System (EKMS). EKMS is the system by which classified and unclassified messages are sent securely to combat units throughout the military. As the program manager, I had a team of 20+ system engineers, software developers, test engineers, and technical writers working to produce updated versions of CUAS created to address software vulnerabilities and to take advantage of new equipment and satellite-based delivery systems.

It was a whole new world for me, as I was not a software person by any stretch of the imagination when I left the Air Force. Fortunately, as always, I worked with some smart, patient people who brought me along to where I became familiar with the technical aspects of the program. I also benefitted from the 2009 passage of the Post-9/11 GI Bill, which provided tuition for veterans who wanted to go to school after leaving the military. That fall, I jumped right on this opportunity.

Over the next four years I earned an Associate's degree in Computer and Information Science from Mesa College (one of the San Diego Community Colleges) and a certificate of proficiency in Project Management from the University of California San Diego. This two-year degree helped provide me with some academic basics I needed to know so I could converse intelligently with my team and with our military customers about computers and software development. The PM certificate, along with experience I gathered at work, helped me gain the knowledge to become certified as a Project Management Professional (PMP).

Largely because of success with the CUAS program, I was promoted to San Diego Site Lead for our division in June 2013, shortly before the company split in two. I went with the portion of SAIC that changed its name to Leidos Corporation. In 2015, I voluntarily transitioned to a consulting employee role at Leidos and began looking seriously at becoming an author.

I am grateful to SAIC/Leidos for taking a big chance on a 52-year-old Air Force colonel with no software engineering experience. One of the many things that attracted me to this company was the way it emphasized quality and integrity, which I have found to be true throughout the organization all this time. I also very much enjoyed working with my dedicated, hard-working, and talented colleagues at SAIC/Leidos. *This was where I had to trust my Leidos boss and the Universe as JoAnn and I moved into a new chapter of semi-retirement in 2015.*

<u>From October 2015 to now</u> I've been a consulting employee for Leidos, working on a part-time basis on proposal activities aimed at our government customers. My wife and I have moved from San Diego to Maui to Seattle and back to San Diego, enjoying the opportunity to see our children and grandchildren and the freedom being able to work remotely brings with it. I am now embarking on this new career as an author and speaker, and have even established my own company, "Aim Point LLC" in support of that. I have placed my trust in the Universe as I have done so many times before.

Appendix B

Air Force Ranks and Abbreviations

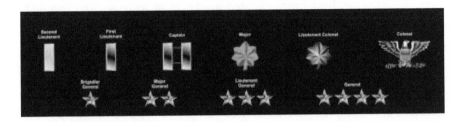

U.S. Air Force officer rank depiction (justom.hubpages.com)

The Air Force is a world unto itself with its own language, structure, and culture. While I've tried to make things understandable throughout the book, it may not be easy to decipher for those who aren't former servicemembers or military enthusiasts. This appendix is a compilation of useful information regarding the Air Force officer rank structure the reader might find useful.

Officer Rank Structure

Rank	Abbreviation	Typical Years of Service	Comments
Cadet	None	4 years before commission	See Note 1
Second Lieutenant	2nd Lt (O-1)	0-2 years of service	
First Lieutenant	1st Lt (O-2)	2-4 years of service	Promotion rate 100% qualified
Captain	Capt (O-3)	4-10 years of service	Promotion rate 100% qualified
Major	Maj (O-4)	10-24 years (maximum)	See Note 2
Lieutenant Colonel	Lt Col (O-5)	15-28 years (maximum)	See Note 3
Colonel	Col (O-6)	20-30 years (maximum)	See Note 4
General Officer	O-7 to O-10		See Note 5

Note 1: Cadets become officers through the Air Force Academy (4 intense years) or Air Force Reserve Officer Training (2, 3, or 4 years concurrent with attending a civilian college). A few officer candidates go through 90-day Officer Training School (OTS). My brother Kevin was an Air Force OTS graduate in 1984. Except in times where the military is expanding rapidly (as during the Reagan buildup in the 1980s), OTS officers are typically former enlisted members or have special technical skills needed by the Air Force.

Note 2: Major is the first promotion that is considered competitive. While the promotion rate for those who meet the board is 85-90 percent, only around 50 percent of the officers commissioned 10 years prior to the board become majors. The difference between these two numbers is that some officers willingly leave the Air Force before coming up for promotion (usually they see better opportunities outside the Air Force). There is also a small number of officers who are asked to leave because of force reduction or substandard performance. Majors typically retire at 20 years, which is the minimum amount of time served to qualify for a small annual pension. Regulations require majors to retire by 24 years of officer service.

Note 3: Lieutenant colonel is the first promotion seen as highly competitive. The promotion rate for those who meet the board is approximately 75 percent. At this point, everyone meeting the board is an accomplished career officer. Only around 33 percent of the officers commissioned as second lieutenants many years before are promoted to Lt Col. Lieutenant colonels typically retire at 20-24 years. They must retire by 28 years of officer service.

Note 4: Promotion to colonel is a combination of dedication, skill, and good fortune. The promotion rate for those who meet the board is approximately 33 percent and everyone meeting the board is a highly accomplished career officer. This means around 10 percent of the officers commissioned as second lieutenants 20+ years before achieve the rank of colonel. The quality of those who compete for promotion is stiff — there are lots of lieutenant colonels who aren't selected for promotion who would clearly make outstanding colonels. Colonels typically retire at 26-30 years and are required to retire by 30 years.

Note 5: There are four general officer ranks in the Air Force: Brigadier General (Brig Gen or O-7); Major General (Maj Gen or O-8); Lieutenant General (Lt Gen or O-9), and General (Gen or O-10). It is ridiculously competitive to get promoted to general officer — only one-half of one percent of the officers in the Air Force are generals of any grade. Brigadier Generals need to retire by 30 years. Higher-ranking generals must retire by 35 years; however, extensions are routinely made for 3- and 4-star generals depending on the positions to which they are assigned.

Appendix C

Eulogy for My Father

Mom and Dad in 1966. They were devoted to each other through 54 years of marriage.

I talk about my father and his impact on my life throughout this book. I believe I best expressed my feelings toward Dad in the eulogy I gave at his funeral in Austin, Texas and his memorial service in Los Altos, California in 1995. He died at age 75 after a three-year battle with prostate cancer. I focused many of my remarks on his military service, as this was a profound connection we had — I was a lieutenant colonel squadron commander at March AFB when he died. My oldest brother, Dave, also eulogized my father, focusing on other aspects of his life. Both of us talked about our love for Dad in his role as our father. Here's what I said:

"It is my great honor to pay tribute to a man who was more beloved and more respected than any man I have ever known. While my father was many wonderful things to me and to all of us who loved him, it is my privilege to represent two very important parts of his life: his service to his country as a dedicated Air Force pilot and officer, and his devotion to his family as a loving father and husband.

"To know my father is to understand the deep patriotism he held as one of his strongest beliefs. While my father would never brag about any of his accomplishments (we always had to drag "war stories" out of him), he was very proud of his career as an Air Force officer. It began in early 1941 as an aviation cadet, leading to pilot wings and a commission as a second lieutenant in the Army Air Corps on September 26th of that year. It was on that same day he married my mother, over 53 years ago. My father was on a troopship headed toward the Philippines when World War II broke out in the Pacific. Diverted to the South Pacific, he fought courageously as a C-47 pilot during the dark days of 1942 and 1943.

"Returning to the United States in 1943, he became commander of the newly formed 314th Troop Carrier Squadron — a very demanding and rewarding position which I believe was the highlight of his military career. He finished his active duty career in late 1945 with the rank of lieutenant colonel — an astounding achievement, even during wartime, for one who was a mere 26-years-old.

"My father continued his Air Force career in the reserves, retiring in 1963 as a brigadier general, a rank only earned by a fraction of one percent of all officers who enter military service. As a combat pilot, he was highly decorated for courage, being awarded the Distinguished Flying Cross three times and the Air Medal on four occasions. Rank and medals, as impressive as they might be, only tell part of the story. Far more important are the wonderful friendships he and my mother made that have lasted over 50 years. As an Air Force commander, at times the most one can hope for is respectful obedience. It speaks volumes about my father that he is so beloved by those serving with him during those difficult years.

"As a parent, my father taught me more than I can ever repay, not that he ever expected anything in return:

> He taught me the joy of unconditional friendship and love.
>
> He taught me to trust in the future and never give up hope.
>
> He taught me to never surrender and 'don't let the bastards get you down.'
>
> He taught me to believe in myself and reach for the sky.
>
> He taught me to never let my airspeed get too low and that if an approach doesn't look good, take the aircraft around — there will always be another chance.
>
> He taught me to 'always keep my options open.'
>
> He taught me not to judge a person on race, religion, sex, or nationality, but only on the character of the individual.
>
> Finally, he gave me the greatest gift a father could ever give a son — he taught me what being a man was all about

"My wife, JoAnn, says it was an honor to know my father. To have him as my dad makes me feel I have been given the greatest blessing a man could hope for. On behalf of my mother, my brothers, and my sister, I want to say 'We love you, Dad. We miss you very much, but we know you are at peace and with the Lord. We pray we will join you in heaven someday because that is where you surely are.'

"Thank you."

Appendix D

Eulogy for My Mother

Mom in the Philippines in 1952. She already had two small children and three more were to come.

My mother died peacefully in early December 2002 as she slept. My relationship with my mother is complicated. Her alcoholism profoundly affects my memories of her. Yet, she was so much more than that. As with my father, my brother Dave and I both gave eulogies at her funeral in Austin, Texas in 2002. I believe the eulogy I gave sums up my love for Mom and does a good job of describing her loving qualities. I was a colonel stationed at United States European Command in Stuttgart, Germany at the time:

"Good morning. It is my great privilege to stand here this morning and tell you about my mother, Ann Cornell Hurd.

"My mother would want all of us to be happy — you all know that. That's the way she was. So, I'm going to start out with a joke.

"In a recent poll about things people fear, death came in second place. Number one was public speaking. Which means many of you would rather be my mother right now, lying in her casket, rather than me standing in front of you talking about her.

"How do I describe my Mom? Many words and feelings come to mind. She was giving to all: family and friends, young and old, those she has known her whole life and those she has just met. Her giving was all without obligation and she was one of the most generous people I've ever known.

"Along with this, my mother was a very trusting soul. Her motives were always honest, and she naturally expected others to treat her the same way. This was one of her great strengths. She kept her positive and trusting attitude toward others throughout her entire life, sometimes despite evidence to the contrary.

"My mother was intelligent and curious. A professional teacher with a master's degree in special education, she was always an avid reader and could speak on a wide variety of subjects. Even during her last few years when she was not mobile and didn't get out much, she still followed world events and the San Francisco Giants in the World Series with equal enthusiasm.

"My mother was adventurous. How else would you describe a Fort Dodge girl who followed her husband to post-war Manila in the Philippines, full of shortages and short on comfort, and love it? She travelled extensively with my father and made close friends throughout the world.

"My mother was a collector of things. Plates, Lladros, Disney figurines, Zolan paintings, you name it, she collected it. For those of you who have looked in her garage on Windmill Road or saw the small storage building my Dad constructed next to the house in Los Altos, you know what I'm talking about. I'm sure the Franklin Mint Collectibles Exchange and numerous dealers throughout the United States are in mourning at my mother's passing, as are we. In all seriousness, her penchant for collecting speaks to my mother's great enthusiasm and joy for life, which I will talk about in a minute.

"I believe, above all else, my mother wanted to love and be loved. It showed abundantly in how she would instantly bond with children whether she knew them previously or not. It showed in how she would always welcome our friends with open arms. It didn't matter whether it was a pal at grade school or an Air Force buddy, she always made them feel like family. My mother's abundant love showed clearly in how she treated the five of us as unique and very important individuals. Most of all, my mother showed her love in her wonderful relationship with my father. He was her heart's desire from the day they met through their 54 years of marriage and beyond. And the truly beautiful thing about their love for each other was that my father shared her feelings every bit.

"To talk about my Mom, we have to center on my Dad — the two of them shared a very deep and powerful love for each other. As with every great love, their relationship was complex at times. Because Dad was such a profound success, Mom often found herself living in his shadow and, while she adored him, I believe there was some envy there.

"The truth is that while Dad was the leader of our family, our strength, and our foundation, my mother was our heart. From my mother, we learned to express ourselves. We learned to laugh freely and give each other great big hugs. From her, we learned the great joy of having our friends over for a party. Whether it was a birthday party or a Little League celebration, a drama club get-together or a 'Bruce is home on leave' party, she made hundreds of events, big and small alike, very special.

"Her warmth and love and friendship drew people to our home like a magnet. Neighborhood friends would invariably come to our house to play and my mother loved it. She didn't care we wore a big bald spot in the lawn where home plate was — she just wanted us to be happy.

"My mother and father together taught the five of us the value of honesty, working to achieve our goals, and loving one another. And while my father was the strong and sturdy rock upon which our family was built, my mother was the unbridled, unquestioning spirit of love and joy which allowed each of us to go many places, do many things, knowing whatever happened, we always had a home to come back to where we would find a joyous welcome as if we were the most important person in the world. And when you were with my mother, to her you were the most important person in the world.

"While we all dearly love my mother and we'll miss her tremendously, today is a time for celebration. We celebrate my mother's love for all of us and our love for her. We celebrate all the many gifts, both real and spiritual, that she gave us. And, above all else, we celebrate her great joy, for she has been reunited with the one, greatest love of her life. As sure as I stand before you, I know that the first face my mother saw, the first voice she heard as she passed peacefully into the next life on two strong legs free of pain, was from a handsome man who welcomed her with his big smile and open arms. And as they joyfully embraced, he said to her 'Hello, Ann, my love. Welcome to heaven. I've been waiting for you.'"